I KNEW WILLIAM BOOTH

An Album of Remembrances

Edited by
R.G. Moyles

CREST BOOKS

The Salvation Army National Publications
615 Slaters Lane
Alexandria, Virginia 22313

© 2007 by The Salvation Army

Published by Crest Books
The Salvation Army National Headquarters
615 Slaters Lane, Alexandria, VA 22313
Major Ed Forster, Editor in Chief for National Publications and National Literary Secretary
Phone: 703/684-5523
Fax: 703/684-5539

Available from The Salvation Army Supplies and Purchasing Departments
   Atlanta, GA – (800) 786-7372
   Des Plaines, IL – (847) 294-2012
   Long Beach, CA – (800) 937-8896
   West Nyack, NY – (888) 488-4882

Printed in the United States of America

Library of Congress Control Number: 2006940281

Photos courtesy of National Headquarters Archives and Research Center, private collection of R.G. Moyles, and The Salvation Army International Heritage Center, London, England

Cover design by Henry Cao
Composition by Judith L. Brown

ISBN 13: 978-0-9740940-9-0
ISBN 10: 0-9740940-9-9

Contents

Introduction

In the late nineteenth century, and well into the twentieth, "William Booth" was one of the most instantly recognized names in the British Empire. As Founder and first General of The Salvation Army – the man whose genius had created the organization and through which he had launched one of Britain's most ambitious social reclamation schemes – his name had consistently claimed headlines in almost every newspaper in the English-speaking world. And the likeness of this tall, gaunt man with the large nose, the silvered hair and long gray beard, either as photo or caricature, could be seen in any number of pictorials and print shops. He was often denounced, and as often praised, but his name and face was always before the people. He was, as one commentator stated, the "most remarkable man living" in late Victorian and Edwardian times.

Enhancing William Booth's visibility was the fact that he traveled more than any man of his day. "He is," wrote W.T. Stead in 1912, "the man who has been seen by the greatest number of human eyes, whose voice has been heard by the greatest number of human ears, and who has appealed to a greater number of human hearts, in a greater number of countries and continents, not only than any man now alive [1912], but – thanks to the facilities of modern travel – than any man who has ever lived upon this planet" (*Fortnightly Review,* 1912). With the exception of 1905, William Booth traveled abroad every year of his evangelistic life. Through Europe almost every year; several-month tours of North America in 1886, 1894, 1898, 1902 and 1907; a six-month tour of South Africa, Australia, New Zealand, India and Ceylon in 1891 and again in 1896 and 1899; state visits with Presidents McKinley and Roosevelt, and Lord Aberdeen; addresses to the United States Senate and Harvard University; an Honorary Doctorate from Oxford University (1907) – all these "peregrinations and profiles" made him world-renowned.

When, in fact, William Booth died in August 1912, he had gained such public respect as an evangelist and social reformer that he was hailed in various quarters as "the greatest apostle of his age," "the greatest revivalist of his day," "the one supremely great religious leader of the nineteenth century" and "one of the most remarkable figures in the religious history of the world." Forgotten were the occasions when he had been branded a "religious fanatic" and "money-grabber," accused of "blasphemy" and "rowdyism," and ridiculed as a "charlatan." Now he was given a place on the pedestal of fame, and accorded an influence equal to that of John Wesley, George Fox, Dwight L. Moody, St. Augustine, Loyola and even St. Paul. He was, many maintained, on a plane with "the greatest philanthropists and Christians of all times."

The reasons for such adulation are twofold. First, his Salvation Army had burst upon an astonished English nation in 1878, fully accoutred with flags, and drums, and tambourines, and "soldiers" in assorted uniforms, "assaulting" sin wherever they found it. A dozen years earlier, in 1865, he and his wife Catherine had decided to spend their religious energy in the service of East London's "unchurched masses" by establishing the East London Christian Mission. It had been a mildly successful venture, had even expanded to nearby cities, but had become bogged down with bureaucracy and entrenched in the rut of orthodoxy. It was his genius, most people believed (not then cognizant of the role his wife had played), that had transformed the rather churchy Christian Mission into the vibrant, military-styled Salvation Army.

"From the moment that the Army received its title," wrote W.T. Stead, "its destiny was fixed." William Booth, now a "general" with complete control and an extraordinary organizational ability, soon had his "soldiers," commanded by "captains" and "lieutenants," regimented into religious action that involved a great deal of marching, with music and banners, and open-air preaching. Enticed into Army barracks, people were treated to an unstructured form of worship that featured lots of singing (many new songs set to popular tunes), plenty of testimonies, short "hell-fire" sermons (couched in the lower-class vernacular), and "instant conversion." The Salvation Army was Wesleyanism in uniform, and it was immensely successful.

So successful that the Army was, in the 1880s, the fastest-growing evangelical organization in Great Britain. Where, in 1877, the Christian Mission had 31 stations, in 1883 the Army had 519 corps; from just 100 officers in 1878, the contingent of full-time preachers grew to 1469 in 1883 (723 male and 746 female); its official magazine, *The War Cry* (commenced in 1879) had a circulation of 100,000 by 1883. By then, more than 200,000 people were estimated to attend Army services each Sunday; and Salvation Army flags had been planted in the United States (1881), Australia (1880), France (1881), Canada (1882), Switzerland (1882) and India (1882). The Salvation Army was a phenomenal success story and, though Catherine Booth was a powerful influence in terms of the Army's theology, William Booth's conspicuous front-line presence, charismatic personality, strong-willed leadership, abundant energy and intense religious commitment made it a reality. And for this accomplishment alone he would, after he had weathered the early criticism, have warranted the praise of the British public.

But a second reason for the adulation was his decision to establish a social wing – to invest his Army with a dual mission – that transformed his reputation as a mere religious leader into one which hailed him as one of Britain's foremost social reformers. In 1890 he published his social manifesto, *In Darkest England, and The Way Out,* wherein he proposed a vast scheme of social amelioration, under three umbrellas: a City Colony, a Farm Colony and an Overseas Colony. The City Colony would rescue men and women from poverty and vice, offering them accommodation and rehabilitative work in Rescue Homes, Prison Gate Refuges, Industrial Centers, and Match Factories. Farm Colony would go a step further by retraining them in agriculture. The Overseas Colony would consist of large, independent Christian farms in South Africa, Canada, or Australia. The *Darkest England* scheme was bold, imaginative and plainly articulated. In the first year William Booth's book sold almost 200,000 copies and helped raise nearly £100,000 to launch his social venture. And for the next two years the "social scheme"– and its colonies – was the subject of everyday conversation because every major newspaper around the world was voicing its opinion on the "scheme," its author and The Salvation Army. And, thereafter, William Booth was known not merely as an outstanding evangelist but as a great public benefactor. Programs like Rescue Homes, Prison Gate Homes, Safety Match Factory, Poor Man's Insurance Society, Social Farms, and Rehabilitation Hostels set new standards for social reclamation.

Therefore, in the years following the "Darkest England Scheme," William Booth began to be much sought after – as a special guest, for interviews and conversations, as a success story, and as the object of personal interest. He continued to be a celebrity – albeit a reluctant one – until his death in 1912, after which many who had known him began to assess his greatness and recall their memories of and acquaintances with him. Together, these recollections comprise an impressive set of snapshots of William Booth – presented here for the first time as an album. They range from very personal memories of those who knew him best, a resident in the Booth home, Jane Short, his son Bramwell, and his first lieutenant, George Scott Railton, to reminiscences by such notable acquaintances and writers as Philip Gibbs, Raymond Blathwayt, W.T. Stead and H. Rider Haggard. They provide not only a remarkable record of personal affection by people who knew and loved him, but also create a revealing portrait of his personality, eccentricities, work habits, family loyalties and spiritual gifts.

While all the authors were, undoubtedly, discerning people, and while some knew him more intimately than others, they are clearly providing *their impressions* of William Booth or recording their opinions at a given moment. One would be unwise to deduce a whole personality from the sum of these parts or to suggest that any part is a true indicator of a very complex personality. But, that acknowledged, they are nonetheless valuable, insightful and rewarding. We can never know the full workings of William Booth's mind, or the deep feelings of his heart, but snapshots such as these bring us a little closer to the man behind the mask of "General" of The Salvation Army.

AT HOME AT HADLEY WOOD

Raymond Blathwayt
in *Interviews* (London: A.W. Hall, 1893): 314-22.

Raymond Blathwayt (1855-1936) began his career as an Anglican clergyman but left the ministry to become a journalist, part-time actor in Hollywood and world traveler. He wrote several books about his travels and acquaintances, the most popular of which was Interviews, *in which he talked with many of the most influential people of his day. The interview with William Booth took place shortly after his Darkest England scheme was launched and around the time when the results of the Eastbourne riots were being tried in various courts. Raymond Blathwayt's interview is therefore quite timely, and his questions elicit some very interesting responses on the part of William Booth. The Booths had moved from Clapton to a new home called Rookstone at Hadley Wood (North London) in 1889. This was about a year before Catherine died. William continued to live there until he died.*

As we entered the small, sparsely furnished sitting room of the very unassuming little villa in Hadley Wood in which General Booth lives, a tall, gaunt figure, clad in a dressing gown which came down to his heels, rose to receive us. This was the great man himself, the originator, the controller, the commander of one of the most marvelous organizations, social, religious, or political, that has ever been known upon this earth. This was the man who rules as with a rod of iron an army that contains within its ranks almost every known nationality; the man who in a moment of time can place his finger upon a village in India, a town in America, a settlement in Australia or the Cape, a hamlet in Great Britain, and tell you to a nicety the number of his followers, the minds and characters of them, their hopes and their prospects, and the work that is done by them in each place. Such a man,

1

it goes without saying, and such an Army, must exercise not merely a great religious, but also a vast social and political influence upon the face of the whole earth. And as I looked upon the curiously-garbed figure, the marked and mingled air of asceticism and ecclesiasticism which so vividly differentiates him from the ordinary run of his fellow Christians, comfortably jogging along upon their heavenward path, and listened to the rapid flow of the words of a man in whom common sense and marvelous insight into the great social problems of the day are far more to be noted than mere eccentricity or fanaticism, I felt that it would be well if I should endeavor in my conversation to elicit, as far as I was able, the political possibilities of such an organization as that which goes to the making up of the much sneered at, little understood, and yet world-conquering Salvation Army. At first the General sat very quietly in his chair and told me of his recent tour around the world, and especially of his brilliant reception in India, during the relation of which, with the reins in my hands, I kept him as far as possible in the political tracks.

"Then General," said I, "after so many brilliant triumphs I may take it that you are becoming not only a great religious leader but even a great political influence in India?"

"Certainly you may," replied the General, as he sprang up and began pacing the floor with long, impatient footsteps, "certainly you may. For though the feeling in India is most friendly to us, yet it is not manifested so much in any general converting work as in a gradual change of attitude towards the English. The Rajahs subscribe to our work, listen to what we have to say, and consider us in a very special manner as the friends of India. I have no hesitation in saying, that while they have always admired and respected Englishmen, we are the first whom they have really loved, and if love is the strongest form of cement, we shall gain them. India is to be ruled by love, not fear. The highest among the native rulers recognize the humanizing work of the Salvation Army. "We think," say they, "that the British are good, but that they are here for their own benefit, not for ours; but the Salvation Army is here exclusively for us, and so we are grateful and we love them." You see, good as many of the English missionaries are, yet they have not learned the great truth that to do real lasting benefit to these people, an

Englishman must not live apart from them, but among them. He must become part and parcel of their lives. To go on the principle that expensive European luxuries are indispensable creates an entire living apart from the people whose souls they have come out to save. The keen-sighted Hindu smiles at this and doubts. My people live on a small pittance each a month, the very life of the country, and so win their way forever to the heart of the great nation. It was the knowledge of all this that caused Ahmedabad, with a population of 120,000 – not fifty persons of whom were even nominal Christians – to turn out in a vast mass of enthusiasm and affection, greeting me with shouts of joy and salaams, and garlanding me with flowers. We are hoping to obtain a large piece of land, on which we will make a large industrial colony, and so prepare India to migrate from the overcrowded parts. All this I explained to the Viceroy, who was delighted, for to him the increase of population is the great problem which he cannot solve and which we trust we shall."

"And do you think you will be able to carry out this policy of imperial federation in Australia, for instance, as well as in India?" I asked the General.

"I most earnestly hope so," he replied, as he took up his position on the hearth rug, tucked one hand beneath the long dressing gown which gave him so ludicrously the air of General of the Jesuits clad in his cassock, while he stretched out the other to better emphasize the exceeding energy of his remarks (for he was now full upon the warpath, and no man could stop him) – "I most certainly hope so. As far as the working population in Australia is concerned, we are a great federating influence, and perhaps the greatest religious force with which they have hitherto come into contact. Our discipline, the simplicity of our aim, the unity of our action, all help to make us a great antidote to anarchy and red socialism. We teach obedience, and we are the only people on the face of the earth except the Roman Catholics, whom with all their errors I greatly respect for that very reason, who do systematically and as part of the plan of salvation teach obedience. Now the new politician says, and he says it nowhere more loudly and persistently than in Australia, 'Everybody must have votes – paupers, prisoners, and lunatics even.' This is contrary to divine law and common sense; the wisest and best only ought to rule. As a matter of fact the whole thing is wrong because of the innate selfishness of the human race," and here for a time the General soared from the region of practical politics into the dazzling empyrean of an impossible altruism. "The king is all for his throne," cried he, "the aristocrat for his class, the plutocrat for his money bags, the working man for himself; then come my submerged tenth, and then chaos! That is the rule of self. Nowhere more clearly shown than in Australia, where the working man is selfishly desirous of retaining the whole land to himself. 'I don't care for your perishing submerged,' says he, 'I want all this for myself.' The labor party there doesn't seek to destroy, I must say that for them, but only to keep. But I trust I have half converted them. New Zealand, for instance, with the most radical government on earth, has offered me a vast tract of land."

"Well now, General Booth, how do you, who are so strong an upholder of law and order, justify the riotous proceedings of your followers at Eastbourne?"

He flung out his long arm at me as he replied, "We go in for righteousness, and on those lines which we see most likely to secure it. If we were in Mashonaland we should accommodate ourselves to the regulations of the country, and so gain our end. If the law of Great Britain forbade our marching with a band on Sunday, we should not do so. Your church missionaries go to China against the wish of the people. But you forbid *us* to go to Eastbourne. We fall back on the common law of this country as expounded by the Lord Chief Justice, who says that we have as much right to march through the streets, bands playing and colors flying, as have Her majesty's soldiers themselves. This has been endorsed by the government, when it repealed the Torquay Act. We shall show them how fair and reasonable we can be when we get our way, as we are quite sure to do. I can bring half the chief constables of England to show that we are the friends of law and order, and we shall be so more and more."

"I am glad to hear it," I replied, "because at times it has struck the more thoughtful of the community that success was turning your heads and destroying the simplicity of your lives and your aims."

"The very reverse," said the General, "we were never more beset with difficulties than today. Our very success makes our difficulties.

The humble spirit and the self-sacrifice of The Salvation Army are greater than ever. Those who don't know our work can have no idea of the agony of it, or the strain upon our nerves. But the joy of it keeps us going. Ah! If only people knew all we went through they would not say the unkind things they do about us. I hear, for instance, that my recent welcome home has terribly offended some people."

"Well," I replied, "that is one of the very things that apparently vexes the righteous soul of my friend [him] here."

Whereupon the General turned smartly round, and said to his secretary, "Well, now, I shall be very much obliged if you will tell me what it is you object to?" They forthwith plunged into a long argument, into which it is unnecessary I should follow them entirely. Said the General: "My people spent six shillings each out of their own pockets to come and meet me, and welcome me home again. But even out of that demonstration and subsequent meeting we cleared £750, with which we are going to start a small hospital for our sick people. We always make money, not spend it, over our demonstrations. I don't cost my people the value of a plum cake. And then again," continued the energetic General, as he turned from my now thoroughly convinced and satisfied companion and continued his conversation with myself, "then again the people grumble at me because I am 'a self-advertiser' forsooth, who is never happy unless he is forcing himself before the public. But, my friend, if you want to make a great political or commercial success you *must* advertise. Publicity in all such cases means success. It is the same with us; and I'll be bound to say I have got more religion into the newspapers over my return, and into the House of Commons over Eastbourne, than has been known for years. The State, aye, and the Church too, will come to recognize me and my Army as their best friends before they have done with us. Just as in India we are turning the hearts of the natives to regard British rule with affection, just as in Australia we are quietly but effectually combating the strong tendency to anarchy and socialism, so here in England we will aid with all our heart and soul the forces that make for righteousness towards God, and for loyalty to Her Majesty the Queen. Our religion is based on the love of Christ for suffering humanity. And it cannot fail. And we cannot advance the real welfare of men without thereby benefiting humanity itself."

"And you consider all your methods are wise and right. Your choice, for instance, of music hall tunes, your queer advertisements, which sometimes to the uninitiated perilously approach the blasphemous, your noisy processions through the streets?"

The General paused in his restless parade, and looking at me solemnly and quizzically he said, "Don't you think that the *dilettante* intonation, as the poet has it, of the Anglican curate has failed as yet to touch the heart of the great seething masses surging around us? 'The dearly beloved brethren' don't respond as they are expected to respond. Now, I come along with my drums and my trumpets," and here the General marched valiantly around and around the room, beating an imaginary drum and blowing an unseen trumpet, with wonderful *verve* and energy. "I come along and at once I get a large and increasing following. No, if anything, we don't have music hall tunes enough. We are getting too respectable, greatly to my regret."

"And you quite justify, to your own conscience as well as to inquirers like myself, your assumption of the title of 'General,' for you know you are quite as much an autocrat as the Pope or the Czar of Russia."

"Exactly," he replied, "and that is where my success comes in, that is why the Pope is such a great force. He is the *Papa*, the father of his people. I feel that I am right in being the father of my people. But I cannot exercise that power beyond the intelligence and the affection of my people, nor do I wish to do so. My power is based on their confidence; my system calls out all the intelligence that is in them. A man rises with us by force of his merit and the due exercise of his intelligence, and by that and that alone he attains to a position of authority. To teach a man to respect himself is the great thing in this life. This is what we do in the Salvation Army. Ours is a mosaic democracy. With us it is a regular scientific process of evolution, in which only the fittest can hope to survive. And by this system we can never fail to exercise an increasing influence upon the nations of the earth, binding them together with the bands of Christ's eternal love."

The General with daughter Emma, who died in a 1903 train wreck.

AT THE TEA TABLE

Rev. William Knight
The Congregationalist (Feb. 14, 1895): 238-39.

Wherever William Booth traveled he was expected, both as a celebrity and because the Army needed to be promoted, to meet with many public dignitaries, greater or lesser. That was certainly true of his North American tour of 1894-95. After a month-long tour of eastern Canada in September, William Booth visited New York on October 22 and from there traveled west to California, back into Canada, via Victoria, B.C., on January 2 and then again through Canada, making his way to Buffalo, New York, from where he sailed back to England on February 27, 1895. It was a five-month tour during which he traveled nearly twenty thousand miles, through nearly one hundred cities, spoke to approximately half a million people, and attended many private sessions with journalists and influential citizens. One of these sessions was covered by a Congregationalist minister, Reverend William Knight, for his denomination's national magazine, The Congregationalist, *published in New York.*

"**A**men!" said the General aloud, as one of the company finished asking the blessing. "And all the people said Amen – said it so you could hear 'em," continued the long-bearded, gray-haired, stooped-shouldered man at my elbow, looking around at us all, with good-humored relish of his point apparent in his odd eyes and mouth.

The cultured family explained that the General had been teaching them to say, "Amen."

Then he silently pushed aside the delicious cup of hot beef tea at his plate.

"Why, General," broke in several of us at once, "can't you take that? It is so good, try it."

"Don't get onto that talk about what you eat; enjoy it if you like and don't bother me talking about it – it is utterly profitless," came the authoritative, but not unkind, words of that voice which is obeyed almost around the globe in deeds of love the most exacting.

"Well, General, isn't the world getting better?" courageously ventured a guest who was sharing this memorable privilege with me.

"Y-e-s, getting more civilized," in a pleasant, but indifferent, tone of voice.

"Well, what is wrong with the Church?" persisted my genial but earnest friend.

"Now you've got into a big subject," broke out the General, waking up in face and voice.

"Isn't the Church coming out of much of her foolishness?"

"Foolish enough yet – seems to me," he answered, half playfully. "But I'm outside, ask him," pointing to our host.

"What is your thought about our institutional churches?"

"What do you mean," said the veteran, looking puzzled.

We explained.

"O, these tabernacles, with baths and playrooms and so on? Well, do they do it all to get people to the penitent form?"

We said that was substantially the aim.

"Yes, but do they get them there – that is the test – do they get them there? The great danger, I take it, in all this is humanitarianism. No matter how much you do, if you stop short of getting a man's soul saved all is vain – vain. The first great principle is to give deliverance. No amount of amelioration will suffice if you stop short of deliverance."

"O, Mary, is this my tea?" said he abruptly to the waitress, who had put it by him, steaming hot, without attracting his attention. He fell to pouring it, and then went on, resting his head sidewise on his hand, with his elbow on the table as he sipped his tea. "You find folks using religion like Worcester sauce – you have Worcester sauce in this country?"

"Yes, we import it."

"You make religion, many of you, too much like something to flavor and enrich a worldly life, not realizing that religion itself is indeed the very essence of our being, the chief, solid business of life to do God's will. Without this – nothing." And the General was glowing now with earnestness, forgetful of his cooling tea; but he was warming all of our hearts.

"But it is a hard matter to make the better classes – as you call them, the better off classes – it is a hard matter to make the better off classes take this in. The fact is that rich people usually make very poor saints," and he softened the utterance by playfully hiding his eagle face behind his thin hand and eyeing our host.

"Don't spoil a good story for relation's sake," said our host, genially.

"If I were told," he went on, with fascinating vehemence and earnestness, "that my head would come off if I did not convert six people soundly in a month, and I were given a list of thirty better off, respectable people and one of thirty drunkards to select from, with my head at stake, I would *instantly* take the thirty drunkards and say to the others, 'Drunkards and harlots will come into the kingdom before you!'" This last, landing him squarely on an utterance of Jesus, was spoken with electric effect.

Then we pressed our line of questions about applied Christianity one point further. "What value do you set on municipal regeneration, good citizen movements, suppressing agencies of vice, Dr. Parkhurst's work, and so on?"

"Oh, that all helps; it does good. We ourselves have done much here and there to shut up vile places, notably an outrageous place in London. Yes, all this helps, but the thing that counts is to get men saved. Now suppose I had gone into some special scheme, total abstinence, for instance, instead of salvation work. Do you think my life would have counted for the world's betterment as it has? My salvation scheme is the best temperance reform in the world, with ever so much more beside. Get men saved – I don't care how you do it – but nothing short of that counts."

"General, you told us yesterday that a man may not know many things in the Bible and yet be a saved man. You said a man might not know about creation and it made little difference, for all the doctors are disputing among themselves about that; a man might know little about the deluge, or be ignorant as to whether Noah's ark and the ark of the covenant were the same; a man might have no idea of Bible history or geography and yet be a thoroughly saved man and know he is saved. Now tell us, please, what part the Bible plays in your work of saving men?"

Leaning toward me, with his elbow on the table and his long fingers pointing at me, and fixing his indelible gaze on me, he said, "I do not bring men to a book – I bring them to *God*." And he sat gazing at me in silence. "God is as real as a book to a man's heart. The head is not the point at which God makes himself known after all. He does not say, 'Give Me thine head,' but, 'Give Me thine heart.' I bring men face to face with God. I make men pray. God says it is not by word, and so on, but by My Spirit. So I don't set men to reading a book, but I bring them on their knees – bring them to God. The Spirit is at work now as surely as when holy men of old spake as they were moved by the Holy Spirit. I make men pray – that does the work. You ministers don't make enough of this. I tell a man to pray – whatever comes first; I want to make him face God. Once a drunkard yielded to my urging, clasped his hands and finally said, 'O Lord, jump straight down my throat and drive the devil out.' What would you have done with him? Anyhow, he is a saved man now. That was about what he needed."

"Don't your people study the Bible?"

"Yes, they read it, often in public, and expound it some. But often they don't understand it. One of my dear men, saved by God's grace, came to 'Alpha and Omega,' and boldly read it, 'I am apples and oranges,' and it meant a good deal more to some of them than if he had read it right. We don't form Bible classes; we find they lead to divisions and disputing. But I believe in the Bible from end to end."

"What of Swedenborg and the danger of vagaries by letting men loose?" I asked, to give a symptom of my own soundness.

"O, poor muddled head, he did untold mischief, but he's righted long before this." And without any show of anxiety for the solidity of his iconoclastic views he sat with a cracker pressed on his lower lip, where he could nibble it.

Have Swedenborg and such as claim to get personal and direct influences quite aside from the Bible really done more harm or gone much further astray than have many sticklers for the written Word in their efforts to interpret it? After all, is there something solid in this shaggy old apostle of the poor's dictum: "I don't bring men to the book – I bring them to God."

"Why, sir," broke out the General, "the greatest triumphs of Christianity were made when there was no New Testament canon, weren't they?"

"But," said our friend who asked the blessing, "that was at a time when men could give personal testimony of what they had seen or heard, or else had received from those who knew first hand."

Quick and glowing was the General's answer. "Yes, and now, today, my precious people can give, do give, just as direct, as real, testimony, and absolutely what they have seen and heard. I set them talking – round the world. I say, tell what has taken place in you. Tell what *you* know, what you *know*. I fix them on the deeper meaning of that word know, know, know, which runs all through the New Testament. No man knows the truths of religion in the New Testament sense when he has only seen them in a book. That comes only as the work of the Holy Ghost in his own heart. Then he knows it, whether he knows Isaiah or John or Paul said so or not. Oh, this putting a book into a man's hands! God is as real and far mightier than a book. Put the man into God's hand. Make him pray. Let us have five minutes of it now."

Down he went on his knees, the waitress stepped back from her duties, the refined table company all bowed, and he began. Softly, earnestly, trembling from head to foot, with his long arms on the table and his hands clasped, he prayed as if now, at last, he had got to the food he relished.

For each of us he prayed like a gracious patriarch. I shall never forget my share in that prayer. Two petitions sank and linger bodily in my soul. "O Jesus, Jesus, Jesus! Not only reign but rule; not only reign but rule – not only reign – but rule! O drive from us that dread delusion so widespread that thou canst reign and yet not rule." Then straightening himself up to his full height on his knees and lowering his voice to a most fatherly, tender pleading, he added: "O Lord, watch over the comrades in arms all around the world; uphold the men and women who are standing up for God tonight everywhere; lead my precious people, O my God." As the prayer ended all the people around that tea table said aloud, "Amen!"

I do not bring people to a book – I bring them to God.

GENERAL WILLIAM BOOTH

George Scott Railton
New York *Outlook,* Feb. 22, 1896

*George Scott Railton (1849-1913), a rather impetuous Methodist preacher, of-
fered his services to William Booth in 1872, after he had read* How to Reach
the Masses With the Gospel, *believing that he and the Booths shared an intense dislike of ecclesiasticism. The Booths, initially reluctant, soon saw his
potential as a preacher, a thinker, and "go-anywhere, do-anything" kind of
person. Almost immediately he became the Mission's secretary, lived with the
Booths for almost a decade, and grew essential to the success of the Army,
writing many promotional pamphlets. He was like a son to Mrs. Booth, while
he and William had an "on-again, off-again" kind of relationship. In 1880 he
pioneered the work in the United States, but was recalled in 1881. After that
he traveled extensively and had charge of efforts in Germany and France. He
wrote a short biography of William Booth in 1912. The piece below was published in the American weekly,* The Outlook, *which a few years earlier had
been a Baptist newspaper called* The Christian Union. *It appeared with two
other articles, one on the Army in general and one on the Ballington Booths,
shortly before they resigned.*

Since I have known General Booth intimately for twenty-three
years, during nine of which I lived in his house, and during all of
which I lived in the utmost imaginable fellowship with him, it is
not only an easy but really a delightful task to describe him. His character and his work I shall not pretend to estimate worthily, for both appear to me far beyond the possibility of a just estimate till, say, a
century or two has rolled away.

Never can I forget our first interview. I had offered myself to him,
and he had insisted upon my coming to London, so that he might see

17

me, and that I might see the Christian Mission which he had founded. Somehow or other, I had imagined I should find a venerable, solemn personage. What was my astonishment to discover a middle-aged man, full of vigor, who scarcely ever kept still for two minutes while he talked, who stood up, hand in pocket, just as frequently as he sat down during my conversation, and who was every inch a man of business!

Such was the reverend founder of a mission to the heathen of London, which had then only a dozen meeting places, most of them small and by no means prepossessing in their appearance, their street doors and windows being generally well spattered with dirt and vegetable refuse. Yet when I heard him speak to the people I saw that he was, on the platform, every inch the true minister of religion. In those days, let it be remembered, the Christian Mission stood almost alone in England, at least in the use of the platform for religious speakers. Elsewhere the use of the pulpit, to which I had myself been accustomed, was all but invariable. The Reverend William Booth, however, had already descended entirely from the pulpit, and there was nothing about his style of preaching that would have fitted those elevated boxes. Yet, all the more because he came so near the people, and moved about as freely as in his own house while he talked to them, I felt that he was truly their minister. His care for and knowledge of them, his determination to make them not only hear and understand but agree with and follow him, was manifest in every word, look, and gesture. Everything about him, on or off the platform, indicated the simple purpose of a man who, having got a great object in view, is determined to attain it if he can.

And then I saw, at a glance, his close relationship to all his people. They all evidently stood as much in awe of him as if he were a huge locomotive; and yet the very grimiest, in his working clothes, could stand beside him without feeling any more stiffness or awkwardness than if he were just a fellow workman. A great leader, to whom no one could dare to say a disrespectful or idle word, he was yet so intimately acquainted with the family and business affairs of all who marched regularly under his command that with a word as he passed them in a doorway he could say more to their hearts than a stranger could have put into a long interview.

Of course the growth of the Mission into The Salvation Army soon made it impossible for him to have anything like so precise an acquaintance even with officers as he had with all its people in those days of small things. But nothing gladdens us all more than the fact that no amount of renown or earthly greatness has in the slightest altered our "Father and General" in that continual exhibition of brotherly love which makes him such a favorite with every poor man who comes into close contact with him. He really cares for everybody, and that is the chief reason why he has come to be so widely and fully obeyed.

There could not be a more absurd misconception than that which paints General Booth as a man who has imposed his will upon others. His energy and power of will are, of course, very extraordinary, but his modesty and hesitation with regard to the correctness of his own views, and his eagerness to learn from anybody, were to me always quite as striking. In the early days of the Mission's growth into the Army, when we lived together almost day and night, there was nothing about him that I so disliked as his everlasting unwillingness to insist upon the carrying out of his own view of what ought to be done by the little people, with their "buts" and head-shakings, whose duty it was to follow him. "Wait, and let us see," he would always say, and it was only when practical lessons had forced the dullest to see that his way was the best one that he would make that way the regulation path for the future. It was his patience, his willingness to hear all that everybody had to say, his constant consideration for the weaknesses and ignorances of others, even more than his desperate courage or zeal for the right, that gained for him the hearty obedience of many thousand.

In private as well as in public the General always dealt very largely in similitudes, and one that he used perhaps more frequently than any other in home consultations with Mrs. Booth, his eldest son, now the Chief of Staff, and myself, was deserving of universal attention. "Look," he would say, "at the peep-show man, who goes to captivate the thousands at the fair. If his show were provided with only one row of spy-holes, placed, say, five feet from the ground, he could exhibit only to the six-footer. But he has enough rows of glasses to suit the height of all possible comers, from the little child to the big man, and thus he manages to get all to see what he has to show them." How often he would extinguish all our pleas, for insistence upon some course, or for the use of some phrase in print that he thought all would not at once properly understand, by the remark: "It's your one row of holes again!"

I never had the pleasure of seeing the General in really good health. It was, even in our smallest and easiest days, an extremely rare thing for him to get a good night's sleep. His appetite was generally so poor and his digestive power so bad that it used to be a constant trouble to Mrs. Booth to induce him to eat without incurring the reproach of having made his work or his sleep more difficult. How often have I heard him complain of the "great spread" which the loving care of officers and friends would set before him on his travels – the "great spread" simply being an ordinary square meal! "Oh, if you *would* only let me have a cup of tea and a bit of dry toast, how grateful I should be to you!" he would remark. Since great ocean voyages have become part of his usual yearly program he has set up the custom of a little private tea of this sort, instead of the huge, prolonged dinner included in his passage.

Not that there was ever any leaning towards asceticism on his part. Instead of wishing to get people to fast, he was always on the stretch for some means of getting the poor better fed. Tea meetings were one of the most useful and honored institutions of the Mission from the first, and the General was always glad when he could give Mrs. Booth the cheering assurance that he had eaten a hearty meal anywhere. But he regards eating and drinking as bothersome necessities, to be submitted to for the sake of maintaining the body in health and vigor, rather than to be needlessly indulged in, lingered over, or talked about.

For work is the great guiding star, one might say, of the General's life. He does nowadays at sixty-six a very great deal more than in the first years of our acquaintance, but it is not because he was then less entirely absorbed in his great task, but because the ever multiplying appliances of civilization, and still more the growth and improved efficiency of the Army, enable him to get through more in a day than we could then hope to accomplish in a month. From the very first day I knew him he has just lived entirely to carry on his one business – the salvation of the world.

Of his character as husband and father I will say little. Surely the many of us who have felt how much he can love those who have no personal claim upon him, and even the multitude who have only seen all this as exhibited in his life, can form some sort of estimate of the intensity and depth of his affection for "his own." How much the General endured during the terrible years of Mrs. Booth's last illness, or how much to this day the great blank of her absence haunts his grandest as well as his loneliest hours, God only can ever know. But the triumph of a father who has eight grown-up sons and daughters spending their whole life in carrying out his plans in various parts of the world is too great for one to attempt in one article to describe it, and that triumph is perhaps the fullest description that could be given of the General's private life.

Of his religion, for the same reason, I have little need to write. Is it not written in living battalions across the world? But I will just say that I think we have in the General's private life a picture of the religion of Christ as it really should be lived nowadays. I have never known him to have time to spare for the prolonged prayers and meditations which we read of in the lives of saints of other days. Much less has he had leisure for those profound religious speculations which have, as we think, disgraced the present generation. Believing the Bible as simply as on the day of his conversion, half a century ago, and accustomed always to look upon God as a friend ever at hand to hear and help, the General has been, I think, a man of prayer in the best possible understanding of the word, a man to whom it is just as natural to speak to God in the street or the railway carriage as in a cathedral or a bedroom. And he has convinced others of the truths he proclaims, not by means of highly elaborated argument or much-studied discourse, but by forcing them to treat God as naturally, personally, and fully as he himself has done.

To hear him denounce the sin and unbelief of his hearers, whether they be a crowd of workmen gathered around a railway truck, or an assembly of the elite of a great city in one of its finest edifices, finishing with a call for instant decision in favor of Christ, is to understand at once why he has been so successful and why he is in many circles so much disliked.

If he has held aloof mostly from all sorts of reformatory and civilizing movements, it is not that he lacks interest in them, or appreciation of every honest effort to improve the condition of the people, but that he has little hope from anything that does not lead up, and very quickly, to the transformation of the individual heart and life.

Naturally, the General has been misrepresented and abused as few men have ever been. This could not but be the case with any man who attacks unsparingly the forces of evil. To carry on a great work, large sums of money must be gathered, and the General has succeeded in this as well as in any other branch of his efforts, notwithstanding all the attempts that have been made from time to time to arouse suspicion of his motives, his integrity, or his economy. Intensely sensitive as he naturally is, he felt abuse and slander, especially when they came from the religious press, very acutely for some years, and all the more as they tended always to lessen the Army's opportunities to do good.

His restlessness has perhaps done more in the past and promises more for the future than any other characteristic of his life. Far from any inclination to settle down or cling to long-cherished habits of thought or action, he is never to be found, after any triumph, however great, in a state of contentment, but always full of regret as to the little accomplished, the slowness of our progress, and the blunders of the past.

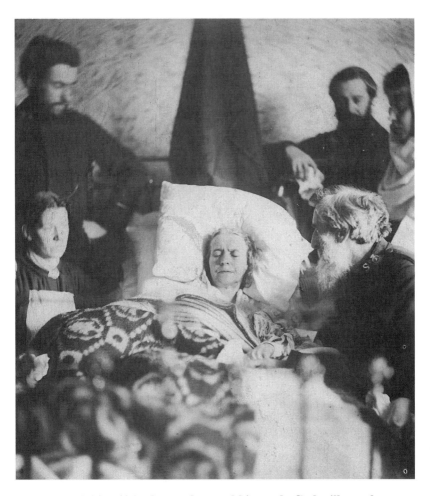

How much his wife's absence haunted him, only God will ever know.

THE MAN AND HIS WORK

Harry Jeffs

Canadian Methodist Magazine, (Jan.-June 1906): 433-41.

A minor writer on religious subjects – such as The Art of Sermon Illustration
– and of one fairly popular emigration book, Homes and Careers in Canada
*(1914), Jeffs was one of many journalists who accompanied William Booth on
the second of his famous motor tours of Great Britain in 1905. The entourage
traveled about 2,200 miles from Folkestone to Glasgow, with the General
speaking to thousands of people in hundreds of towns along the way. Whether
Jeffs accompanied Booth on the whole tour or merely this portion of it is un-
clear. The article below was first published by* The Primitive Methodist
Quarterly *in London and copied by the* Canadian Methodist Magazine.

The famous Boston "Stump," dear in memory to the Pilgrim
Fathers, and a valued landmark to the fishermen of the Wash,
was dimly seen through the gloom as, on a Monday evening in
early September, General Booth's procession of motor cars entered the
ancient East Anglian town. It was my fortune to occupy a seat in the
second car, following the pilot, and immediately preceding the white
car of the General. We had flitted over the eighteen miles from the old-
fashioned town of Horncastle, the whole population of which had
cheered us "goodbye."

All along the road the people were gathered, waving hats and handkerchiefs, mothers holding up their children to see the General. At
every crossroad there was a little crowd gathered from the villages of
the countryside. Laborers rushed to the hedges, and servant men and
maids leaned over the walls of wide-stretching parks. Long will they
remember the passing of the aged General, who waved his hand in ac-
knowledgement of the shouted "God bless yous!"

We entered Boston to find, as it seemed, the entire population waiting to give us a royal welcome. It was with difficulty that a clear space was kept for our passage to the spacious Market Place, and then we had to force our way through a seething human sea into the Corn Exchange, where all the local notabilities were assembled to support the General. This was a sample of the reception that had been given to the General on his journey of two thousand miles from Folkestone to Glasgow and south again.

Talking to Commissioners of The Salvation Army during the two days I spent with the General on his tour, I learned that they and General Booth himself had been continually carried back in memory to the years when the entrance of a band of Salvationists into any town or village was a signal for a disgraceful outbreak of rowdyism such as that which the pioneers of Methodism, and later on the pioneers of Primitive Methodism, almost invariably unwillingly provoked: Now it was "roses, roses all the way." Decoration of the streets, the Town Hall placed freely at the General's disposal, the Mayor, the Corporation, the Magistrates, the County Council Chairman, uniting to give him the heartiest of welcomes, and bid him "Godspeed" in his work. What was the secret of this revolution in public opinion?

Let me relate two personal experiences out of many that I have had which may help to account for the popular, the municipal, and the united churches' welcome to General Booth. I went a year or two ago to Lady Warwick's estate at Easton, near Dunmow in Essex, where about seventy men from The Salvation Army's labor colony at Hadleigh were carrying out extensive works on a contract given by Lady Warwick to the labor colony. These men were busily engaged with spades and barrows in laying out a piece of landscape garden at the back of the mansion. I was invited by the officer in command to go among the men and freely question them.

I discovered among those who were wielding the spades or wheeling barrowloads of earth a doctor of music, who had held a leading position as organist, a former head of a department in a Tottenham Court Road firm who had earned well on to a thousand a year, a doctor, and other professional men, and men who had held responsible positions in business. These men had fallen victim to drinking or to gambling.

Some of them had been in prison. They had lost their characters, lost their means of livelihood, lost their self-respect, lost their friends, and had sunk lower and lower until they were homeless, and physical and moral wrecks.

Then they fell into the hands of an officer of The Salvation Army, or drifted into one of the Army's night refuges for the men who cannot scrape together the fourpence or sixpence for a night's lodging. The Army had had pity on them, sent them to the labor colony, taught them to work, fed them, brought religious influence to bear on them, all the while keeping a tight hand upon them, holding them up until they were able to stand by themselves, and this holding up in such cases is usually a long and weary process.

It is an experience of The Salvation Army that those who have fallen from the greatest heights are the most difficult cases to lift up to any height at all. Men and women who have been educated, who have lived in comfort and refinement, when once they have sunk into the mire have not the muscular or the moral fiber of the men and women who have always lived hard lives, and they seem often hopelessly incapable of making any effort at all for their reformation, and they have to be held for a year, or two years, as a weakly babe is held under the arms, or by the waistband, before they can be trusted to walk alone.

These men assured me of their profoundest gratitude to the Army for what it was doing for them. It was rebuilding the backbone they had lost, it was giving them courage, it was restoring their self respect, and though they might never recover the positions they had lost, yet they realized that they had the opportunity of beginning a new life, in which they might find contentment and happiness. Had the Army not come to their rescue, heaven only knows what would have become of these men.

And the Army has had not only men of this class to deal with, but it has had ministers of all denominations, and clergymen who have held prominent positions in the established Church, but who through drink or other causes have fallen from their high estate into the seething mass of misery known as "the submerged tenth." The Salvation Army has realized its claim to be the moral and social scavenger of the nation.

A week or two later than the motor tour, I went down to the hop fields in Kent where, during the hop picking season, the slums of South and

East London send thousands of their poorest population. I called at an empty house which was occupied for a time by a party of Salvation Army women – social and slum officers. An empty house, I repeat, in spite of this occupation, for the only furniture was a rough table or two and some chairs borrowed from a neighboring schoolroom. These women, eleven in number, had brought with them sacks which they had stuffed with straw, and these sacks were their beds. One of the women remained in the house to attend to the cooking and other necessary domestic arrangements, which were reduced to the lowest possible minimum.

I had a talk with some of these women about their work in the slums, and also in the hop fields, which they regarded as a holiday. The previous week had been a week of almost continual rain, bleak and cold, yet every morning these women had left the house shortly after six, had tramped a forty minute walk to the fields, and there they remained around the clock, working side by side first with one and then another, helping them to fill their bins, hearing their stories, and seizing every opportunity of speaking to them about the Savior who once Himself had no place to lay His head, but was always the Friend of the poorest of the poor. I was told that they had been soaked to the skin, but not one of them had dreamed of abandoning the post of duty. They had met with terribly sad cases. For instance, there was a woman who had left her home with a fifteen-day old baby in order to earn a few shillings at the hop picking, and so help her husband, a consumptive compositor.

Many of the people they tried to help appeared to be hopelessly hardened. They took what service was given them in the way of helping to fill their bins greedily, but without gratitude, and grumbled when the women left to talk and work with others.

"Oh," said one of the officers to me, "it seems as if a thick, dark veil was drawn between many of these people and God, and it seems impossible to lift the veil, but we pray about it, and we believe that God will not let our work be in vain."

Does not such work as I have described at Lady Warwick's estate, and in the hop fields, sufficiently explain the national honor done to William Booth, culminating in the presentation to him at the Guildhall of the freedom of the city of London?

But how has this social work, which is now carried out in all the continents, in about forty countries, evolved out of the purely evangelistic mission with which General Booth began?

Let us return to the meeting in the Corn Exchange at Boston where, for nearly an hour and a half, the General explained the development and the agencies of the Salvation Army. He told how he had been a minister of the Methodist New Connexion, and had been satisfied and happy with doing the ordinary work of a minister until he found himself placed in the east of London. Then he looked around him and was appalled at the poverty, the misery, the demoralization and degradation of the people who were herded together in the East End. He found the people who most needed the uplifting power of the Gospel never entered the churches, and that the ordinary machinery of church work was hopelessly inadequate to bring these people under the influence of the Gospel. He brooded over the problem, and at last the conviction was borne in upon him that a new machinery must be created on entirely novel lines, the means being exactly adapted to the ends to be attained.

One day he conceived the idea of the Salvation Army, and went home to his wife and said, "My love, I have found my work." He explained to her what was on his mind. She heartily endorsed his decision, and the two knelt together and dedicated themselves to the service of God among the poorest and most degraded of the population. He found in his wife, whose memory, next to the example and teaching of the Savior, is his greatest inspiration and spur, an ideal helper.

Mrs. Booth, whom it was my privilege to know during my early years in London, was a woman of the greatest force of character, with a wonderfully clear head, and a genius for organization. General Booth acknowledges that she was the thinker and theologian of the Army during its first quarter of a century of existence, and it is largely due to her that the Army created the host of self-denying women workers who have counted it an honor to toil and beg and starve, if need be, so that the work can be carried on. Mrs. Booth's name will go down in history as one of the greatest and most influential women workers for the extension of the Kingdom of Christ since the days of the Apostles.

The General told the Boston meeting how thirty years ago his health broke, and he was strongly urged to consult a great specialist, and he went on two conditions – that the gentleman who was most pressing in his advice should pay the fee, and the General should be allowed to please himself whether he followed the prescription.

The specialist carefully examined him, and gravely informed him that he might consider his work was done. He should get a quiet country parish, where there was little work, where the air was good, and where there was plenty of fishing and shooting.

"That," said the General with twinkling eye, "was thirty years ago. I did not follow the prescription, but I have had plenty of fishing for men, and have had good shooting at the devil."

To look at the General – tall, thin, with snowy hair and beard – one asks can this frail-looking man be actually in his seventy-seventh year? He looks it. He might almost sit for a picture of Moses in the plains of Moab, blessing the children of Israel before his death. But is it possible that this man should be the Herculean worker who does enough to wear out three men of fifty in the course of ten years? How General Booth can work I saw for myself on the day after that grand entry into Boston. He spoke three times indoors for from an hour and twenty minutes to an hour and a half each time. Not satisfied with this, he spoke three times out of doors for ten minutes or a quarter of an hour each time. Yet at the end of the day he seemed as fresh as if he had traveled without any speaking at all, but simply for the sake of "the glory of motion" and enjoyment of the country air.

This is the era of wonderful old men, but General Booth appears to be still more wonderful in the tireless energy of his grand old age than Mr. Gladstone himself. What is it that keeps him so fresh? The explanation is simple. General Booth, like John Wesley, has one passion only, but it is an overmastering passion. His consuming desire is to do his Master's work in saving the bodies and souls of his Master's people, and it is this ruling passion that keeps him going.

If General Booth ceased work for a month it is the conviction of those who know him best that he would collapse, but he begrudges every moment that is not given to the promotion of the mission which he is absolutely convinced God has given him to do. He regards himself as wholly in God's hands, and so far as he is personally concerned he takes no thought for the morrow, though nobody is more far-seeing than General Booth is in thought for the future of the work he has instituted.

The General loves to have a little chaff at the expense of the press, but nobody appreciates the value of press support to his work more than does General Booth. I heard afterwards what was the usual diet of the General during this long tour. He is rather faddy in some respects, and particularly with regard to his food. He is a vegetarian, and eats remarkably little if anything at all. His supper after an arduous day's work is often simply a rice pudding, to be made without sugar, and a roasted apple.

I was told by the Commissioner who accompanies General Booth on his foreign trips that the General sleeps well, but is at the same time a light sleeper, and frequently wakes up in the night. His active mind is always engaged in planning and scheming for the Army, and his secretary has always to be at his call at any hour of the night to take down from the General's dictation his instructions.

In a talk at the International Headquarters on Queen Victoria Street with General Booth's chief foreign traveling companion I heard that even on board ship bound for Australia or elsewhere the General works almost incessantly from eight or nine in the morning till nine, ten, and even eleven, at night. His cabin is crowded with books and reports relating to the Army's worldwide work. The General has every detail at his finger ends, though he now leaves much detailed work that he used to undertake himself to his son Bramwell and to the able and experienced staff of officers whom he has trained in his methods.

The General studies his books and reports, dictates speeches, sermons and instructions, thinks out new developments, and, in fact, regards every moment as golden, far too precious to be wasted in mere resting. He allows himself now and again a ten-minute constitutional on deck, and after his frugal vegetarian mid-day meal he will take a forty minute nap, and will perhaps sit quietly for a couple of hours afterwards while his secretary reads to him.

On land he will travel journeys of many hours' duration in extreme heat or extreme cold, and at the end appears "as fresh as a daisy." He is a confirmed tea drinker, and his traveling baggage includes a spirit lamp and kettle with which tea can be made *en route*. This is his one luxury.

The General's home is at Hadley Wood, near Barnet, where I had the privilege of spending a couple of hours with him a few days before his departure for Germany. It is very little indeed of his time that the General spends at his home. The house is pleasantly situated, standing by itself, overlooking fields and trees. The modest sitting room in which we conversed has portraits of Mrs. Booth and some of the General's children. One of the portraits was a large photograph of his son-in-law, Commissioner Booth-Tucker, who lost his wife, the General's youngest daughter [actually second oldest daughter], in a railway accident in the United States last year. Commissioner Booth-Tucker has written an inscription on the photograph in which he pledges himself to follow the General faithfully "till death do us part."

The General talked to me about his early life. His father was a fairly well-to-do man, sprung from the farming class, but he had gone into building speculation and did pretty well until in the General's boyhood bad times came and reduced him to comparative poverty. The General was about sixteen years old when he was converted, and he said his conversion completely changed his attitude toward life. Within half a dozen hours of surrendering himself to his Savior he was at work in attempting to save others, going in and out of cottages in the slums of Nottingham delivering a message from his Master to the people.

He began evangelistic work on a small scale, but was unsettled for several years, and it was not till some ten years later that he entered the ministry of the New Connexion Church. He was happy enough in that first circuit of Spalding, but soon found himself cramped in ordinary circuit work, and so began the larger work which developed into The Salvation Army. When he began the Christian Mission in the East End the General did nothing without full consultation with the men who worked under him.

"But I found," he said, "that if I went on in this way we should make no progress. There was so much discussion, so much controversy, so much committee work over every little detail, that we should soon have been brought to a standstill. I called the men together and gave them the option of leaving me or of remaining with me on the condition that they allowed me to plan the work, and they were willing to carry out my orders. I saw that what they had in their minds was to settle down into a sect, while I wanted the work to continually progress and expand.

"At first it was my own idea that the converts should enter into existing churches, but two denominations that I approached placed obstacles in the way of their reception. Then I found that I wanted the converts myself to turn them into officers. When the idea of an Army got accepted it greatly helped the converts to know that what was expected of them was obedience. It is for a General to plan and for a soldier to obey, and this prevented all the friction that would have arisen under other conditions. I had been greatly interested in military biography and came to see that the military organization might be applied with very great effect to religious work.

"They say I am an autocrat. Well, I don't mind that. As a matter of fact, however, there is very little autocracy in The Salvation Army. If an officer shows himself capable he produces his plans, I listen to what he has to say and in nine cases out of ten I tell him to 'go ahead.' If there is anything I see reason to object to we discuss it together. If he can convince me that he is right he has his way, but we do not have much trouble about that."

Talking over the social work, the General told me how it had all arisen inevitably in the most natural way. It began with the opening of a home on the smallest scale for lost girls. These girls were met with in the course of the evangelistic work and something had to be done for them temporarily or would have drifted back to their old life, so the first rescue home was started. Out of that had arisen other homes by means of which something like forty thousand girls and women had been taken off the streets and the vast majority of them had kept straight. In like manner the night shelters for men, the labor "elevators," the prisoners' homes, the farm colonies, and a host of other institutions of all sorts had come into existence.

Working as it does among the very lowest strata of society the Army found it simply impossible to leave these people to wallow in hopeless misery. It would have seemed a mockery to preach the Gospel to them and to make no attempt to lift them out of the mire and to drag them from under the wheels of the chariot of the social juggernaut. The General drew attention to the fact to which I have already referred, that the people rescued are by no means confined to the poorest and ignorant who have been brought up in the slums, but they include an appalling number of men and women who have sunk down from the superior classes. He will not have it either that the officers of the Army are ignorant men and women. "How," he asked, "could men and women destitute of education have created such an organization as The Salvation Army and carried it on with such increasing success? As a matter of fact the officers of the Army include men and women of high social position and of the best education who have been willing to cast in their lot with the Army and work side by side with comrades who have been among the rescued proteges of the Army."

The General spoke in high praise of his women officers. He confessed that at one time he looked askance at the employment of women. He especially disliked women preachers. He was taken, however, to hear a young woman preacher on Fetter Lane, and she preached one of the most striking sermons he had ever heard in his life. That settled the matter with him so far as women preachers and officers were concerned.

As to the foreign work, this also arose inevitably out of the home operations of the Army. Men were converted at Army meetings in England and went abroad, where they started mission work on their own account; or foreigners who happened to be in England got converted and returned to their own countries and started work. The work grew beyond the capacity of its originators to carry it on, and then appeals were sent to the General to supply officers who should take charge of the work on behalf of the Army. A drunken milkman, converted in East London, emigrated to Australia, held a meeting in his house in Adelaide, and the work spread into other Australian centers. The Army was appealed to, sent officers to the Antipodes, and today the Commonwealth government and the governments of all the colonies support the Army in every way as the most powerful social salvage organization of that continent.

The General is looking longingly towards Russia. On the day of my visit he had received a telegram from Finland stating that "Russia is open." He hopes Russia will be entered via Finland, as soon as arrangements can be made, and that The Salvation Army will become a powerful agency in that distracted country. The Army was introduced into Finland by a couple of Finns who went to a Salvationist conference at Stockholm, started a little work of their own in their own country, and then begged the General to have them trained in England and to send them back to carry on the work under the Army's banner.

"I have never," he said, "studied maps to see whether there was a country in which I could start work. I have waited for the country to send for the Army. There are appeals now to which we cannot for the time accede, from countries where work is being carried on which the people claim to be Salvation Army work."

At the time of writing the General is holding meetings in Germany, and is being hailed there with the same enthusiasm, as a great religious and social reformer, as he was on his motor tour in our own country. He is doing a great work for the promotion of international peace. It is no small thing that an Englishman should have started a religious organization which has been able to plant itself in so many different countries, among such widely diverse races, and to train in so short a time native officers to carry on the work of The Salvation Army with such surprising results.

I was anxious to know what training the Army gives its officers. The General was characteristically frank on this point. He admitted that the training had not been what it ought to have been. It had been necessary quickly to multiply officers, and to train them at a minimum of expense. The work had suffered from sending officers after only three or four months training into active service. Now the time of training had been extended to nearly a year following on the training of youthful cadets in the various corps to which they belong throughout the country. The General said: "I cherish the hope of seeing a great Salvation Army University founded, which shall be the center of our training operations, but we must wait till God opens up the way."

What will be the future of The Salvation Army?

Pessimists are plentiful who predict that when the General's strong hand and masterful will are withdrawn, the Army will be ruined by dissension among the ambitious officers, and will collapse like a house of cards. What I have seen and heard from men in the innermost circle of the Army's operations leads me to believe that the Army is a much more stable organization than is commonly imagined. General Booth leaves more and more of the management of the Army's affairs to his son, Mr. Bramwell Booth, and to the extremely able, energetic and devoted headquarters staff which directs the multiplied activities of the Army.

I have been assured by one of the head Commissioners that Mr. Bramwell Booth, though his work has been mostly done out of sight of the public, possesses his father's organizing genius and his father's ravenous appetite and inexhaustible capacity for work. The Commissioners have no doubt whatever that the Army will hold together. The very vastness of its operations and the complication of its organization ensure its permanency.

Certain elements that might have caused dissension and schism have been eliminated or have voluntarily withdrawn themselves, and there remain sifted and tried men whose pride in the Army is no less than that of the General himself. Those men express the most unbounded enthusiasm in the capacity of Mrs. Bramwell Booth, who, as director of the women's social work, and as a spiritual force in the Army, is little less influential than was the General's wife herself.

The General's motor tour, in which he was accompanied by his principal officers, did very much to bind the officers closer together. No break-up of the Salvation Army is feared so long as the Army's work continues along the progressive lines on which it is now conducted. If there were to be slackening down, a settling into ruts, and a disinclination to adapt methods to new conditions, then, indeed, there might and would be trouble, but then The Salvation Army would cease to be The Salvation Army, and a new Salvation Army would have to be created. The remainder of the General's life will probably be spent as the traveling world missionary of The Salvation Army.

A word should be said, in conclusion, as to the Methodist element in the Salvation Army. Undoubtedly the Army owes its existence to the fact that General Booth was a Methodist. It was in Methodism that he served his apprenticeship as organizer, and learned how to make the best of untutored but enthusiastic men and women. It is the Methodist theology of personal experience of salvation, the theology of the love of God, the theology of the Gospel of Jesus Christ as the only thorough and permanent reforming agency, that has been the mainspring of The Salvation Army organization.

The General, at his great meeting on the motor tour, in the presence of local magnates and of the ministers and clergy of all denominations, including Roman Catholic priests, Anglican rectors and Unitarian ministers, never forgot to point to the crucified Savior as the one hope of a ruined and a dying world.

Our forefathers who, in the early days of our denomination, did the work which we have left too much to The Salvation Army in the later days, would have recognized in General Booth a kindred spirit. Let us not be too proud to learn lessons from The Salvation Army, and especially let us endeavor to re-catch from The Salvation Army the old Gospel, the old spirit, and the old willingness to bear and to do anything and everything, regardless of what respectable people think, if only we can reach the lost and bring them to their knees at the foot of the cross.

All along the road people were waving hats and handkerchiefs.

AT QUEEN VICTORIA STREET

A.G. Gardiner

Prophets, Priests and Kings (London, 1908); rpt. London:
Dent, 1914: 186-94.

Alfred George Gardiner (1865-1946), well-known journalist and author, was editor of the London Daily News *from 1902 to 1919. He launched his literary reputation with the popular book,* Prophets, Priests and Kings, *which provided sketches of most of the prominent persons of his time. William Booth's inclusion in the book indicates just how prominent a person he was. A.G. Gardiner's assessment of William Booth's success is based on several interviews held with him and on Mr. Gardiner's acquaintance with The Salvation Army.*

When William Booth rises to receive you in his office at Queen Victoria Street, the first impression you have is of the alertness of the lithe, lean form in its frogged coat with the legend "Blood and Fire" blazing in red letters below the reverend white beard. The second impression comes from the eye. Certain men live in the memory by the quality of the eye alone. That was so in the case of Gladstone. His eye obsessed you. It seemed to light on you like a living thing. It penetrated you like a sword and enveloped you like a flame. It was as though he seized you in his masterful embrace and swept you whither he would. You did not question: you obeyed. No man who ever fell under the compelling hypnotism of that imperial and imperious eye will ever forget it. General Booth, too, dwells in the memory by the eye. It does not dominate you as Gladstone's did, but it fascinates you by its concentration. It searches the thought behind your words. It seems, with its beady brilliancy, to be burrowing in the dark places of your mind. You feel that your secret, if you have one, is being unearthed. You are sapped and mined. Your defenses are crumbling beneath that subtle assault. There is nothing for it but flight or surrender.

You emerge from the interview with a new and revised version of the General. You went in to meet a saint and a visionary. You come out having met the astutest businessman in the city. You feel that if the tradesman's son of Nottingham had applied himself to winning wealth instead of winning souls he would have been the Rockefeller of England. He would have engineered "corners" and "squeezes" without precedent. He would have made the world of finance tremble at his nod. When he passes by the Stock Exchange he must say: "There, but for the grace of God, goes William Booth."

His genius for affairs is visible in the vast fabric of his creation. The world has seen nothing like this movement that in one brief generation has overspread the earth with a network of social and regenerative agencies. You may question its permanence, you may doubt its methods; but as an achievement, the achievement of one man, it is a miracle.

It astonishes by its absolute independence of motive and origin. Loyola's Society of Jesus sprang organically out of the Roman Church; Wesley to the end regarded his movement as a movement within the Church. But The Salvation Army is unique. It has no relationship with any church or any system. Like Topsy, "it growed." It is an empire within the Empire. It is a system without a dogma and without an intellectual interpretation. It is, in fact, a revival movement converted into an organism.

It is a miracle which could only have been performed by an autocrat, and General Booth is above everything an autocrat. "L'état? C'est moi." His whole career is a record of absolute reliance on the leading of his own spirit. This quality revealed itself even as a boy of sixteen, when, left fatherless with the burden of a business upon him, he cut himself adrift from the Church of England, in which he had been baptized and brought up, and took to street preaching. He had been inspired by the visit to Nottingham of the American revivalist, James Caughey, whose straightforward, conversational way of putting things, and whose common sense manner of forcing his hearers to a decision, seized his imagination. He allied himself with Wesleyanism, gave up business, and began his campaign, gathering his crowds in the street, wet or fine, taking them to the penitent form inside, reaching the poor and the outcast if in no other way than by songs and shouting. Wesleyanism was shocked by these improprieties. It sought to make him respectable. He found himself, in his own phrase, "hooked into the ordinary rut and put on to sermon-making and preaching."

He refused to be respectable. He cut Wesleyanism and tried Congregationalism. He found it bookish and intellectual and turned to the Methodist New Connexion, of which he was ordained a minister fifty years ago. But again the fetters of restraint galled him. He was put on circuit work instead of the revival work he passionately desired. The final emancipation came at the Liverpool Conference of the Connexion in 1861. Once more, despite his appeals, he was allocated to circuit work. "Never!" said William Booth. "Never!" echoed the voice of his wife from the gallery. And so, at thirty-two, without a penny of assured income, and with a wife and four young children to support, he faced the world, a free man.

And when his movement began to emerge from Mile End Waste, amid the brickbats of the Whitechapel mob and the hideous caricature of the Skeleton Army, the same masterful spirit prevailed. He found his ideas hindered by the conference, and the conference vanished like a Duma at a wave of his hand. Not even his family must break his iron law. His son desired to remain in America beyond the term allowed for service – insisting on remaining. Then his son must go. Do you question the future of the Army? The future is provided for. I, the General, have named my successor. "Who will it be? No one knows but me. Not even the lawyers know. His name is sealed up in an envelope, and the lawyers know where to get it. When my death is announced the envelope will be opened and the new General proclaimed."

It is magnificent – it is war. There is the key to the mystery. It is war. It is still the custom in some quarters to ridicule the military aspects of the Army. It is inconceivable that the insignia and discipline of militarism can have any literal application to the spiritual realm. The thing is a travesty. We sing "Onward, Christian Soldiers," but that is only a poetic simile, and the Christian army sits in comfortable pews outside the range of fire. General Booth conceived a literal warfare, his battleground the streets, his Army uniformed and disciplined, challenging the world with fierce war cries, its principle unquestioning obedience. It is necessary to remember this when we charge him with being a dictator. An army in the field must be ruled by a dictator, and his is an army in the field.

"They call me a Pope sometimes," he says. "I reply it is the only way. Twenty people are banded together, and nineteen are for taking things easily, and if you leave them to themselves they will take the easy path. But if you say 'Go; that's the path,' they will go. My people now want and wait to be commanded." His mistake is in supposing that a dictatorship can be bequeathed. Cromwell made the experiment and the Commonwealth vanished. A system which derives all its vitality from a personality may fade when that personality is withdrawn. For the Salvation Army is not a church or a philosophy or a creed; it is an emotion.

An emotion! You look in that astute eye, so keen, so matter-of-fact, so remote from the visionary gleam, and ask for the key to the riddle. And the truth dawns upon you that there is a philosophy behind the emotion. When the artful politician sets out on an adventure he appeals to the emotion of patriotism or to the emotion of hate of the foreigner and fear of the unknown. So General Booth has a practical purpose behind the spiritual emotion. He is, in a word, a politician. He is a social reformer working through the medium of spiritual exaltation. Wesley saw only the Celestial City, and he called on men to flee from the City of Destruction. General Booth points to the Celestial City, and he uses the power generated by the vision to drain the City of Destruction and make it habitable. He is as designedly political as any socialist, for it is the redemption of society in the material as well as the spiritual sense that is his aim. But politics in the party meaning are forbidden to his followers as absolutely as alcohol. Change the laws by all means, he says to the politician, but I am working to change the heart. "We are tunneling from opposite sides of the hill. Perhaps we shall meet in the middle."

He has the enthusiasm of humanity. He loves mankind after the fashion of the philanthropist. The average man is touched by the incidental and particular. His pity is casual and fleeting. His heart goes out at the moving tale; he feels for the sorrow he sees. But he is cold to misery in the mass, and generally shares the conviction of the northern farmer that "the poor in a loomp is bad." The philanthropist, on the other hand, is often cold to the particular, but he has that imaginative sympathy that bleeds for the misery of the world. His pity is not casual; it is a frame of mind. His eyes look out over wasted lands; his ears ring with lamentation and an ancient tale of wrong. He is not so much indifferent to the ordinary interests of life as unconscious of them. General Booth's detachment from the world is as complete as if he were an anchorite in the desert. He has a single purpose. "The one prudence in life," says Emerson, "is concentration; the evil one, dissipation." General Booth has the concentration of the fanatic – the fanatic governed by the business mind. He carries no impedimenta. Politics are a closed book to him; the quarrels of creeds are unheard; literature unknown; his knowledge of golf is confined to a suspicion that there is such a game.

Yet he is the most familiar figure in all the world. He has traveled further and spoken to more diverse peoples than any man in any time – to Hindus by the sacred Ganges, to Japanese by the sacred mountain, in Germany often, in America and Australia and New Zealand. He flashes from Land's End to John O'Groats in a motor car, whips across to Berlin, is heard of in South Africa. Yet all the time he seems to be in the bare room on Queen Victoria Street, talking eagerly as he walks about and stopping at intervals to take you by the lapel of the coat to emphasize a point. All this activity bespeaks the ascetic. "Any amount of work can be performed by careful feeders," says Meredith; "it is the stomach that kills the Englishman." General Booth is careful of his stomach. He lives the life of a Spartan. His income has never exceeded that of a curate, for it is wholly derived from a fund of £5000 invested for him years ago by an admirer – a fund which returns to the benefactor after the General's death. From the Army he draws nothing beyond traveling expenses.

His indifference to the judgments of the world has in it a touch of genius. It is not easy to be common. Religion, like society, suffers from the creeping paralysis of respectability. The General set himself to shock the world by being common, and he rejoiced in the storm he created. He had nothing to do with the world of proprieties and "good form." His task was to reclaim the abyss, where the methods of organized Christianity were futile. "My work is to make war on the hosts that keep the underworld submerged, and you cannot have war without noise. We'll go on singing and marching with drums beating and cornets playing all the time." It is the instinct of the businessman – the instinct of advertisement applied to unselfish ends. He is the best showman of religion. "I would stand on my head on the top of St. Paul's cross if I thought it would bring men to salvation."

Intellectualism has no place in his life. Theology he leaves to the schools and the churches, and "modernism" is a word that has no meaning for him. Metaphysics are not a path to the masses, and his answer to the "new theology" would be "Hallelujah!" His creed is like Holmes'. "I have a creed," said Holmes. "It is summed up in the first two words of the Paternoster. And when I say them I mean them." So with the General. "The religion of the Army is summed up in the two great commandments, 'Thou shalt love the Lord thy God with all thy heart,' and 'Thou shalt love thy neighbour as thyself.'" He applied no other formula. The dogmas will take care of themselves. "A man tells us he is a good Catholic? Are you true to the principles of your faith? And so with the Protestant." His banner is as broad as the heavens.

His methods are his own, and he will bend them to no man. He never argues; he simply goes on as if he did not hear. "I shall not reply to Mr. Dowie. I leave my work to speak for me. We must both answer to the Great Judge of all." He is charged with sweating, with not paying the trade union rate of wages. What are trade unions to me or I to trade unions? He seems to say. I am saving the lost; I am setting their foot on the ladder; stand aside. His finances have been constantly challenged, but he will not disclose them. Yet his personal probity has never been impugned, and when in 1892 the agitation came to a head and a committee consisting of Sir Henry James, Lord Onslow, Mr. Long and others was appointed to investigate the facts, it found that no member of his family had ever derived any benefit from the money raised for his *In Darkest England* scheme, that the administration had been "businesslike, economical, and prudent," and that the accounts "had been kept in a proper and clear manner." He is charged with indifference to the source of his money. "I was once reproached with having accepted a donation of £100 from a well-known Marquis. 'It is tainted money,' they said. What if it was? Give us the money, I say; we will wash it clean with the tears of the fatherless and lay it on the altar of humanity."

He has the unconquerable cheerfulness of the man who lives for a cause and has no anchorage in things or possessions. "My wife is in heaven and I have no home, merely a place where I keep some furniture," he says; but no man I ever met is less weary. He has that dauntless spirit of youth. "How old do they say I am? Seventy-nine? What nonsense! I am not old. I am seventy-nine years young. I have heaps of time yet to go around fishing – fishing for souls in the same old way with the same old net." He is like an idea, an enthusiasm, that lives on independent of the flesh. The flame of the spirit flares higher as the candle flickers to the end. He will go out with a burst of "Hallelujahs" and a roll of drums.

Wesleyanism was shocked by his improprieties.

THE MAN WHO HUNGERED
FOR HELL

Leigh Mitchell Hodges
New York *Outlook* (Sept. 26, 1908): 175-78.

The following article in one of America's most prestigious weekly news maga-
zines was most likely written in anticipation of General Booth's fifth, and fi-
nal, visit to North America in 1907. He was then in his seventy-ninth year and
very much a world statesman rather than a mere evangelist. Leigh Hodges is,
therefore, in reviewing the life and achievements of William Booth, very re-
spectful and laudatory, and, though more incisive than most journalists who
wrote about him, borders on the eulogistic in his appraisal.

"I hungered for hell. I pushed into the midst of it – London's East Side. For days I stood in those seething streets, muddy with men and women, drinking it all in and loving it all. Yes, I loved it because of the souls I saw. I knew I had found my work. One night I went home and said to my wife: 'Darling, I have given myself, I have given you and our children, to the service of those sick souls.' She smiled and took my hand, and we knelt together. That was the first meeting of the Salvation Army."

His tired eyes, their cunning half curtained by great drooping lids, blazed with blue flame as he spoke. His voice, a remnant of departing thunder, rumbled like a distant storm in summer. But all is winter now with this old soldier of salvation – all save the spirit. The tousled hair and streaming beard which frame his huge face – they are the hoar frost of nine and seventy years. That enormous hooked nose is the beak of an eagle, a man-eagle long since sated with the sublimities of the thin

51

upper strata and swooping down to snatch broken bodies and scorched souls from the ash heaps of humanity. Tall, spare, unsteady, his is the body of Doré's Don Quixote with the head of Ezekiel set upon its stooped shoulders. Did he claim reincarnation, he might call himself Ezekiel. There is much likeness. He is somewhat the fierce benefactor. His cry is Ezekiel's – Work and Hope! He knows all filth, all grief, all horrors, yet he sees the sunrise. Surrounded by dust of defeat and degradation, smoke of sin, fog of falseness, and clouds of crime, he has shown men a patch of Christ's clear morning sky on the horizon of hopelessness, as he marched on through the wide world dragging them out of darkness and death into light and life. He is sure of his providential mission. Who knows but this possibility confronted him in his Methodist pulpit fifty years ago! He was only fifteen when he heard an echo of that voice which smote Paul on the road to Damascus. Even then he preached as if possessed. William Booth was possessed.

He hungered for hell. He thirsted for dregs. A little while he waited. He had enough of routine religion to breed the hope that these would come to satisfy his longing. Waiting, he worked and thought. One day it came to him that Christ "sought" men when here. He, too, would "seek" them, but not on the highways. He would track them into the swamps and sinkholes, the dump-heaps. For this he led his little family to London in 1861. For this he haunted the nearest approach to hell on earth – the East Side. For this he knelt with his wife, a woman of blessed memory everywhere. He always lifts his eyes when he calls her name, as if speaking to her.

Mind you, he was not a failure, seeking fresh soil in which to thrive. His fame as an evangelist was high and fixed. He could have gotten a comfortable living from any conference. He was a schemer, planning a factory where waste material could be utilized and saved.

In an abandoned cemetery on Mile End Road he pitched an old tent. The sentimental will see in this a sign of resurrection from the dead. He chose the place because he could get no other. The tent was his tabernacle. He called it the "Christian Mission." A crowd of poor Whitechapelers drifted into the place the first night he preached, led by curiosity. The East Side had never seen such a "congregation," nor London, nor the world, for that matter. It was just a mess of wreckage cast up by the waves of what we must call life because of breath and heartbeats. He talked to them as such. He told them the old, old story stripped to the quick of its layers of theology. He worded his message to fit their meager knowledge. Some slept through it all; some sneered and snickered; others listened. A harlot or two and a drunkard cried for shame at their sinning and then for joy at their saving, and thus ended the second meeting of what was yet to sweep over seas as the Salvation Army. William Booth went home tired but happier than he had ever been. He had won from the devil at the first throw.

He seized the spoils of this skirmish. They not only went to work with him, but he went to work through them. In their needs he saw the needs of their kind. He saw how the ears of the devil had grown stony to sounds of church bells which sifted into that part of London. He would go at the devil with drums, and he did.

And the godly world that had somehow neglected this human offal shifted into its high seats and frowned. Then, when bands of his people went through the streets singing about Jesus of Nazareth to the tunes of "Sally in our Alley" and "The Old Stone Jug," that godly world, which still held well aloof from the field, fumed at such sacrilege. Its pious respectability was outraged by this "charlatan." Spurgeon let fly a shaft at this "fanatic," saying his methods brought religion into contempt. Huxley joined the chorus and dubbed his Christianity "corybantic." Yet you see today, gathered together under the generalship of this same William Booth, the biggest standing army in the world – only it doesn't stand. It forges ahead, fighting, and winning wherever it fights.

"In the last few years we have saved fifty thousand fallen women," said this General to me. He sat up straight in the car seat, and the light on his face was something more than the reflection on the gold-leaved trees past which the train was rushing. "They say such women cannot be saved; that they have fallen too far. Women fall farther than men only because they slip from greater heights. I wish I could show them these fifty thousand as they *were* and as they *are*!"

He doesn't care for the honors and compliments heaped upon him by kings and emperors. To dine with Roosevelt doesn't ruffle him in the least. I warrant you he let Oxford "doctor" him last year more for the sake of not displeasing the old university than pleasing himself. But if he could marshal his fifty regiments of reclaimed womankind before you or me! – that would fill him with satisfaction. The way he spoke showed it.

And if he could only find some way to work while he sleeps! – that would make him smile. He seldom smiles, yet he is witty and knows fun when he sees it. "Twenty years ago an English physician told me I was worn out. He said I ought to retire to some small parish and spend much time fishing and shooting. God had already given me one of his small parishes – this world – and I have found excellent fishing everywhere, only I have caught mostly crocodiles. As for shooting, I'm still firing at the devil, and if I've not yet hit him in the head, I've wounded him several times in the tail." He told this during his recent illness, while making his fifth tour in our country.

He believes in a personal devil, indeed he does. He snarled when I asked him, and, taking for granted I differed in the matter, growled at "your microbe devil." He believes in a sure-enough hell, too, but he balks at the brimstone. He avoids particulars as he avoids disputes about religion.

"I've no time to argue theology," he says. "Whether Christianity is right or wrong, you must admit it is the most wonderful force that has ever come along." He will go one step farther, and after that you might as well try to whistle against a hurricane. "There are three things one must have: Forgiveness of the past, strength to be good in the future, and a spirit of love for others. If there is any way to get these except through regeneration by the Holy Ghost, I have yet to find it. Now we have talked enough about religion."

Criticized as he was at first by those of every creed, you cannot draw from him a word of countercriticism for any creed.

"Men need many roads to salvation, and it takes all my time and thought and energy to keep the one I opened in repair."

He gives it just that – all his time, thought, and energy. Sometimes he awakes at daylight and calls his secretary to take down a thought, a message, an order. On shipboard he has a specially constructed chair in which to write while sitting on deck. During his recent illness he was vexed beyond measure because he was unable to work on trains and in hotels. He was petulant, like a boy kept in after school – wondering when he could make up his lost time. He wanted to go on with his latest effort, the preparation of messages or brief sermons, written to be translated into every language conquered by the Army, and read simultaneously at its services throughout the world Sunday after Sunday. He finished forty before his strength gave out. Even then he kept at his tour, despite the doctors, and met every lecture date. It was forced draught and you could see the steam getting low. "I haven't had a day off in fourteen years," he told a group of newspapermen in Philadelphia, "but I'll die pretty soon and the first thing I'll ask for in heaven is six months' vacation!"

Immensely practical, General Booth has carried this crusade into fifty-three countries, leaving nothing to chance and mighty little to providence; grappling with conditions instead of arguing theories; feeding the hungry and sheltering the homeless; clothing the naked and tending the sick; visiting those in prison and befriending the friendless – doing it "unto the least of these" and doing it all for one reason – for Christ's sake.

"Do not call it philanthropy," says General Booth; "it is all a means to an end, and that end is the salvation of the individual." Yet he does not regale you with the number of souls he has "saved." Instead he tells you that last night twenty-two thousand men and women were given shelter by the Army, and "last night" is any night. He tells you that ten times that number were fed by the Army last week, and "last" week is any week. He tells you how in each of his rescue missions is hung this sign, printed in bold black letters: "Before Committing Suicide Apply to the Captain." It was his New Year gift to humanity in 1906, this scheme for decreasing self-destruction. Of the first five hundred who "applied to the captain" in London only two took the fatal step. The others got a fresh hold through sympathy or sane advice, and in a few instances were given funds enough to sand the track for a new start.

He tells you of the Army's "transfer of population" work, how they are making farm fits out of city misfits; how they are helping men and women by leading them out of temptation; how they are shifting thousands from the narrow streets of London to the airy prairies of western Canada; how they are mending men here, there, and everywhere – but never boastingly, always "by God's grace"; how, by God's grace, they are now at work upon a plan for helping the lonely.

"Loneliness. Did you ever think what sorrow and sin come of it?" he asks. "In every city are thousands of lonely persons, not always poor, but without family or friends. They have no place to go where a friendly spirit may be found. We want to give them clubs where they can get this, where they can find congenial work if they wish it." This is the Army's first move in any field apart from the "mud and scum of things." It has always done much for the rich, however. This among prodigal sons and daughters. It has been the great "lost and found" column for such wanderers, and thousands of times has it returned them to woebegone parents, not only safe and sound, but fitted for the line of duty. So it has worked for the rich as well as the poor. It never questions the pocket, but the plight.

From that crude beginning in the deserted burying ground it has branched in all directions, blossoming in the blue pokebonnet and the visored cap in nearly every country under the sun. From the one officer who braved the scorn of many it has increased to more than twenty-one thousand officers, who command the respect and the admiration of the majority. Its many-sided work is directed from eight thousand posts, each garrisoned by a corps whose one purpose is the serving of sick souls through the most direct means.

See and hear the old warrior at its head, and you have the human secret of its vast success. Read the last twelve verses of the twenty-fifth chapter of Matthew, and you know the rest. The eagle face and the towering form seem already to reflect the light of another morning. The first glow of the final sunrise falls athwart this mountain of a man who hungered for hell. When he answers the last roll call, there can be read over him no better tribute than this, printed a few months ago in the Nagoya Daily News, a Japanese journal professedly Buddhist: "It was not the physical poverty and hunger of London slums that made him forget his wrecked constitution and pledge his whole life to his new field of activity. It was the miserable condition of the souls of men and women, and his burning desire to save them from eternal destruction, that set fire to his intense love for mankind."

Three things one must have are forgiveness, strength, and love.

IMPRESSIONS OF
WILLIAM BOOTH

H. Rider Haggard
Regeneration (London: Longmans, 1910): 208-17

Henry Rider Haggard (1856-1925) was an English novelist and social activist, best known for his romantic novel King Solomon's Mines *(1885). His reputation as a noted agriculturist gained him service on several government commissions concerning agriculture for which he was knighted in 1912. In 1905 he was appointed by the Colonial Office to inquire into The Salvation Army's farm colonies in the United States with a view to establishing similar land settlement colonies in Great Britain. Though the report was shelved, he nevertheless produced a book called* The Poor and the Land, *which dealt favorably with the Army's effort. Later William Booth asked him if he would write a report on the Army's social work in Great Britain for publication in book form. He agreed to do the work for nothing except expenses and later gave the copyright to* Regeneration *to The Salvation Army. William Booth, after reading the book, wrote to him: "I have just read* Regeneration. *It is admirable. You have not only seen into the character and purpose of the work we are trying to do with the insight of a true genius, but with the sympathy of a big and generous soul. From my heart I thank you." Mr. Haggard's "Impressions of William Booth" are placed at the end of the book, as a way, he says, of making known the man who brought the vast social enterprise into existence.*

It has occurred to me that a few words descriptive of William Booth, the creator and first General of The Salvation Army, set down by a contemporary who has enjoyed a good many opportunities of observing him during the past ten years, may possibly have a future if not a present value.

Of the greatness of this man, to my mind, there can be no doubt. When the point of time whereon we stand and play our separate parts has receded, and those who follow us look back into the gray mist which veils the past; when that mist has hidden the glitter of the decorations and deadened the echoes of the high-sounding titles of today; when our political tumults, our town-bred excitements, and many of the very names that are household words to us, are forgotten, or discoverable only in the pages of history; when, perhaps, the Salvation Army itself has fulfilled its mission and run its course, I am certain that the figure of William Booth will abide clearly visible in those shadows, and that the influences of his work will remain, if not still felt, at least remembered and honored. He will be one of the few, of the very few enduring figures of our day; and even if our civilization should be destined to undergo eclipse for a period, as seems possible, when the light returns, by it he will still be seen.

For truly this work of his is fine, and one that appeals to the imagination, although we are so near to it that few of us appreciate its real proportions. Also, in fact, it is the work that should be admired rather than the man, who, after all, is nothing but the instrument appointed to shape it from the clay of circumstance. The clay lay ready to be shaped, then appeared the molder animated with will and purpose, and working for the work's sake to an end which he could not foresee.

I have no information on this point, but I should be surprised to learn that General Booth, when providence moved him to begin his labors among the poor, had even an inkling of their future growth within the short period of his own life. He sowed a seed in faith and hope, and, in spite of opposition and poverty, in spite of ridicule and slander, he has lived to see that seed ripen into a marvelous harvest. Directly, or indirectly, hundreds of thousands of men and women throughout the world have benefited by his efforts. He has been a tool of destiny, like Napoleon, only in this case one fated to help and not to harm mankind. Such, at least, is my estimate of him.

A little less of the spirit of self-sacrifice, a different sense of responsibility, and the same strength of imagination and power of purpose devoted to purely material objects, might have raised up another multi-millionaire, or a mob leader, or a self-seeking despot. But, as it happened, some grace was given to him, and the river has run another way.

Opportunity, too, has played into his hands. He saw that the recognized and established creeds scarcely touched the great, sordid, lustful, drink-sodden, poverty-steeped masses of the city populations of the world; that they were waiting for a teacher who could speak to them in a tongue they understood. He spoke, and some of them have listened; only a fraction it is true, but still some. More, as it chanced, he married a wife who entered into his thoughts, and was able to help to fulfill his aspirations, and from the union were born descendants who, for the most part, are fitted to carry on his labors.

Further, like Loyola and others, he has the power of rule, being a born leader of men, so that thousands obey his word without question in every corner of the earth, although some of these have never seen his face. Lastly, nature endowed him with a striking presence that appeals to the popular mind, with a considerable gift of speech, with great physical strength and abounding energy, qualities which have enabled him to toil without ceasing and to travel far and wide. Thus it comes about that as truly as any man of our generation, when his hour is ended, he, too, I believe, should be able to say with a clear conscience, "I have finished the work that Thou gavest me to do"; although his heart may add, "I have not finished it as well as I could have wished."

Now let me try to convey my personal impressions of this man. I see him in various conversations with myself, when he has thought that he could never make use of me to serve his ever-present and impersonal ends, trying to add me up, wondering how far I was sincere, and to what extent I might be influenced by private objects; then, at last, concluding that I was honest in my own fashion, opening his heart little by little, and finally appealing to me to aid him in his labors.

"I like that man; *he understands me!*" I once heard him say, mentioning my name, and believing that he was thinking, not speaking.

I tell this story merely to illustrate his habit of reflecting aloud, for as he spoke these words I was standing beside him. When I repeated it to his officers, one of them remarked horrified:

"Good gracious! It might just as well have been something much less complimentary. One never knows what he will say."

He is an autocrat, whose word is law to thousands. Had he not been an autocrat indeed, The Salvation Army would not exist today, for it sprang from his brain like Minerva from the head of Jove, and has been driven to success by his single, forceful will.

Yet this quality of masterfulness is tempered and illuminated by an unfailing sense of humor, which he is quite ready to exercise at his own expense. Thus, a few years ago he and I dined with the late Mr. Herring, and, as a matter of fact, although I had certain things to say on the matters under discussion, his flow of most interesting conversation did not allow me much opportunity of saying them. It is hard to compete in words with one who has preached continually for fifty years!

When General Booth departed to catch a midnight train, for the continent I think, Mr. Herring went to see him to the door. Returning presently, much amused, he repeated their parting words, which were as follows.

General Booth: "A very good fellow – Haggard; but a talker, you know, Herring, a talker!"

Mr. Herring (looking at him): "Indeed!"

General Booth (laughing): "Ah! Herring, you mean that it was I who did the talking, not Haggard. Well, *perhaps I did."*

Some people think that General Booth is conceited.

"It is a pity that the old gentleman is so vain," a highly placed person once said to me.

I answered that if he or I had done all that General Booth has done, we might be pardoned a little vanity.

In truth, however, the charge is mistaken, for at bottom I believe him to be a very humble-minded man, and one who does not in the least overrate himself. This may be gathered, indeed, from the tenor of his remarks on the subject of his personal value to the Army, that I have recorded at the beginning of this book ["in short, he had no fear that the removal of his own person and name would affect the organization."]

What people of slower mind and narrower views may mistake for pride, in his case, I am sure, is but the important and unconscious assertiveness of superior power, based upon vision and accumulated knowledge. Also, as a general proposition, I believe vanity to be almost impossible to such a man. So far as my experience of life goes, that scarce creature, the innately, as distinguished from the accidentally eminent man, he who is fashioned from nature's gold, not merely gilded by circumstance, is never vain.

Such a man knows but too well how poor is the fruit of his supremest effort, how marred by secret weakness is what the world calls his strength, and when his gifts are in the balance, how hard it would be for any seeing judge to distinguish his success from common failure. It is the little pinchbeck men, whom wealth, accident, or cheap cleverness has thrust forward, who grow vain over triumphs that are not worth having, not the great doer of deeds, or the seer whose imagination is wide enough to enable him to understand his own utter insignificance in the scale of things.

But to return to General Booth. Again I hear him explaining to me vast schemes, as yet unrealized, that lurk at the back of his vivid, practical, organizing brain. Schemes for setting tens of thousands of the city poor upon the unoccupied lands in sundry portions of the earth. Schemes for great universities or training colleges, in which men and women might be educated to deal with the social problems of our age on a scientific basis. Schemes for obtaining government assistance to enable the Army to raise up the countless mass of criminals in many lands, taking charge of them as they leave the jail, and by regenerating their fallen natures, saving them soul and body.

In the last interview I had with him, I read to him a note I had made of a conversation which had taken place a few days before between Mr. Roosevelt and myself on the subject of the Salvation Army. Here is the note, or part of it.

Mr. Roosevelt: "Why not make use of all this charitable energy, now often misdirected, for national ends?"

Myself: "What I have called 'the waste forces of Benevolence.' It is odd, Mr. Roosevelt, that we should both have come to that conclusion."

Mr. Roosevelt: "Yes, that's the term. You see the reason is that we are both sensible men who understand."

"That is very important," said General Booth, when he had heard this extract. "Make use of all that charitable energy, now often misdirected for national ends! Why not, indeed! Heaven knows it is often misdirected. The Salvation Army has made mistakes enough. If only that could be done it would be a great thing. But first we have got to make other people 'understand' besides Roosevelt and yourself."

That, at least, was the sense of his words.

Once more I see him addressing a crowded meeting of city men in London, on a murky winter afternoon. In five minutes he has gripped his audience with his tale of things that are new to most of them, quite outside of their experience. He lifts a curtain as it were, and shows them the awful misery that lies often at their very office doors, and the duty which is theirs to aid the fallen and the suffering. It is a long address, very long, but none of the hearers are wearied.

At the end of it I had cause to meet him in his office about a certain matter. He had stripped off his coat, and stood in the red jersey of his uniform, the perspiration still streaming from him after the exertion of his prolonged effort in that packed hall. As he spoke he ate his simple meal of vegetables (mushrooms they were, I remember), and tea, for, like most of his family, he never touches meat. Either he must see me while he ate or not at all; and when there is work to be done, General Booth does not think of convenience or of rest; moreover, as usual, there was a train to catch. One of his peculiarities is that he seems always to be starting for somewhere, often at the other side of the world.

Lastly, I see him on one of his tours. He is due to speak in a small country town. His officers have arrived to make arrangements, and are waiting with the audience. It pours with rain, and he is late. At length the motors dash up through the mud and wet, and out of the first of them he appears, a tall, cloaked figure. Already that day he has addressed two such meetings besides several roadside gatherings, and at night he must speak to a great audience in a city fourteen miles away; also stop at this place and that before he gets there, for a like purpose. He is to appear in the big city at eight, and already it is half-past three.

Five minutes later he has been assisted onto the platform (for this was before his operation and he was almost blind), and for nearly an hour pours out a ceaseless flood of eloquence, telling the history of the organization, telling of his life's work and of his heart's aims, asking for their prayers and help. He looks a very old man now, much older than when first I knew him, and with his handsome face and long, white beard, a very type of some prophet of Israel. So Abraham must have looked, one thinks, or Jeremiah, or Elijah. But there is no weariness in his voice or his gestures; and, as he exhorts and prays, his darkening eyes seem to flash.

It is over. He bids farewell to the audience that he has never seen before, and will never see again, invokes a fervent blessing on them, and presently the motors are rushing away into the wet night, bearing with them this burning fire of a man.

The Founder received an honorary Doctor of Civil Law from Oxford.

THE OLD PATHFINDER

Harold Begbie

The Daily Chronicle, August 22, 1912

Harold Begbie (1874-1929) began his career as a newspaperman, first contributing bits of verse to the Daily Chronicle *and then writing a column for the* London Globe. *His book of Boer War poems,* The Handyman, *rivaled Kipling's in its patriotic appeal. He then began writing very successful novels, and later turned to a keen interest in social issues to produce several highly popular books on the social inequality of the times. Among them were* Broken Earthenware *(1910),* In the Hands of the Potter *(1911), and* Other Sheep *(1911), all featuring, to a greater or lesser degree, the work of The Salvation Army. Begbie was, therefore, not only sympathetic to Booth's mission, but very familiar with it and with Booth himself (he had also accompanied Booth on one of his motor tours of Britain). He became intimately acquainted with both when, in 1920, he wrote his monumental, two-volume* Life of William Booth. *In spite of its worshipful tone, it still stands as the best biography of Booth that has been written. The eulogistic piece below was written at the moment of William Booth's death in 1912.*

Scarcely could you find a country in the whole world where men and women are not now grieving for the death of General Booth. Among people of whom we have never heard, and in languages of which we do not know even the alphabet, this universal grief ascends to heaven – perhaps the most universal grief ever known in the history of mankind.

One realizes something of the old man's achievement by reflecting on this universal grief. It will not do to dismiss him lightly. Moreover, it will not do to express a casual admiration of his character, an indulgent approbation of his work. The man was unique. In some ways he

69

was the superman of his period. Never before has a man in his own life-time won so wide a measure of deep and passionate human affection.

It will not do to say that by adopting garish methods and appealing to people who are outcasts. General Booth established his universal kingdom of emotional religion. Let the person inclined to think in this way dress himself in fantastic garments, take a drum, and march through the streets shouting "Hallelujah." There is no shorter cut to humility. Many have tried to do what William Booth did. Many men as earnestly and as tenderly have sought to waken drugged humanity and render the kingdom of heaven a reality. Many men have broken their hearts in the effort to save the Christian religion from the paralysis of formalism and the sleeping sickness of philosophy. It is not an easy thing to revivify a religion, nor a small thing to rescue many thousands of the human race from sin and misery.

Let us be generous and acknowledge, now that it is too late to cheer his heart, that General Booth accomplished a work quite wonderful and quite splendid, a work unique in the records of the human race. Let us be frank and say that we ourselves could have done nothing like it. Let us forget our intellectual superiority, and, instead of criticizing, endeavor to see as it stands before us, and as it really is, the immense marvel of his achievement. Our canons of taste, our notions of propriety, will change and cease to be. The saved souls of humanity will persist forever.

I remember very well my first impression of General Booth. I was young, I knew little of the sorrow of existence, I was perfectly satisfied with the traditions I had inherited from my ancestors, I was disposed to regard originality as affectation, and great earnestness as a sign of fanaticism. In this mood I sat and talked with General Booth, measured him, judged him, and had the audacity to express in print my opinion about him – my opinion of this huge giant, this Moses of modern times. He offended me. The tone of his voice grated on my ears. His manner to a servant who waited upon him seemed to me harsh and irritable. I found it impossible to believe that his acquaintance with spirituality was either intimate or real. Saints ought to be gentlemen. He seemed to me a peculiar old man, a clumsy old humorist, intolerant and fanatical.

Later in my life I met him on several occasions, and at each meeting I saw something fresh to admire, something new to love. I think that he himself altered as life advanced; but the main change, of course, was in myself – I was able to see him with truer vision, because I was less sure of my own value to the cosmos, and more interested to discover the value of other men. And I was learning to know the sorrows of the world.

There is one very common illusion concerning General Booth. The coarse sneers are forgotten, the scandalous slander that he was a self-seeking charlatan is now ashamed to utter itself except in vile quarters; but men still say – so anxious are they to escape from the miracle, so determined to account for every great thing by little reasons – that his success as revivalist lay only in his powers as an organizer. Now, nothing is farther from the truth. General Booth was not a great organizer, not even a great showman. He would have ruined any business entrusted to his management. He would long ago have ruined the organization of the Salvation Army if his life had been spent on that side of its operations. Far from the hard, shrewd, calculating, and statesmanlike genius of the Army's machinery, General Booth has always been its heart and soul, its dreamer and its inspiration. The brains of the Army are to be looked for elsewhere. Bramwell Booth is the man of affairs. Bramwell Booth is the mastermind directing all those worldwide activities. And but for Bramwell Booth the Salvation Army as it now exists, a vast catholic organization, would be unknown to mankind.

General Booth's secret, so far as one may speak about it at all, lay in his perfectly beautiful and most passionate sympathy with suffering and pain. I have met only one other man in my life who so powerfully realized the sorrows of other people. Because General Booth realized those sorrows so very truly and so very actually, he was able to communicate his burning desire for radical reformation to other people. The contagiousness of his enthusiasm was the obvious cause of his extraordinary success, but the hidden cause of this enthusiasm was the living, breathing, heart-beating reality of his sympathy with sorrow. When he spoke to one of the sufferings endured by the children of a drunkard, for instance, it was manifest that he himself felt the very tortures and agonies of those unhappy children – really felt them, really endured them.

His face showed it. There was no break in his voice, no pious exclamation, no gesture in the least theatrical or sentimental. One saw in the man's face that he was enduring pain, that the thought was so real to him that he himself actually suffered, and suffered acutely. If we had imagination enough to feel as he felt the dreadful fears and awful deprivations of little children in the godless slums of great cities, we, too, should rush out from our comfortable ease to raise salvation armies. It would be torture to sit still. It would be impossible to do nothing.

This wonderful old man suffered all his life as few have ever suffered. And his suffering arose from the tremendous power of his imagination. At a meeting he would tell amusing stories, and in the company of several people he would talk with a gaiety that deceived; but with one or two, deeply interested to know why he was a Salvationist and what he really thought about life, he would open his heart, and show one at least something of its agony. He was afflicted by the sins of the whole world. They hurt him, tore him, wounded him, and broke his heart. He did not merely know that people suffer from starvation, that children run to hide under a bed at the first sound of a drunken parent's step on the stair, that thousands of women are friendless and defaced on the streets, that thousands of boys go to their bodily and spiritual ruin only for want of a little natural parental care, that men and women are locked up like wild beasts in prison who would be good parents and law abiding citizens were love allowed to enter and plead with them – he did not merely know these things, but he visualized and felt in his own person the actual tortures of all these perishing creatures. He wept for them. He prayed for them. Sometimes he would not sleep for thinking of them.

I have seen him with suffering face and extended arms walk up and down his room, crying out from the depths of his heart: "Oh, those poor people, those poor people! – the sad, wretched women, the little, trembling, frightened children meant to be so happy! – all cursed by sin, cursed and crushed and tortured by sin!" And he would then open his arms as if to embrace the whole world, and exclaim, "Why won't they let us save them?" – meaning, "Why won't society and the state let The Salvation Army save them?"

His attitude towards suffering and sorrow was, nevertheless, harder in many ways than that of certain humanitarians. He believed in a devil, he believed in hell, and he believed in the saying that there are those who would not be persuaded though One rose from the dead. And so he held the wisdom of statesmanship that when all men have been given a fair opportunity for repentance, and after love has done everything in its power to save and convict the lawless and the bad, those who will not accept salvation should be punished with all the force of a civilization that must needs defend itself. The word punishment was very often on his lips. I think that he believed in the value of punishment almost as profoundly as he believed in the value of love. He believed that love could save the very worst man and the very worst woman in the world who wanted to be saved; and he also believed that nothing was so just and wise as rigorous punishment for the unrighteous who would not be saved. I think that he would have set up in England, if he had enjoyed the power which we give to politicians, two classes of prison – the reforming prison, controlled only by compassionate Christians who believe in love; and the punishing prison, which isolates the evil and iniquitous from contact with innocence and struggling virtue. In that direction this most merciful man was merciless.

Why he became a Salvationist is very clear. He knew that the center of life is the heart. He saw that all efforts of statesmanship to alter the conditions of existence must be fruitless, or, at any rate, that the harvest must be in the far distant future of humanity, while the heart of man remains unchanged. He suspected the mere respectability which satisfies so many reformers. Even virtue seemed to him second-rate and perilous. He was not satisfied with abstention from sin or the change from slum to model lodging house. He held that no man is safe, no man is at the top of his being, no man is fully conscious of life's tremendous greatness until the heart is definitely and rejoicingly given to God. He was like St. Augustine, like Coleridge, and all the supreme saints of the world in this insistence upon the necessity for a cleansed heart and a will devoted to the glory of God; he was different from them all in believing that this message must be shouted, dinned, trumpeted and drummed into the ears of the world before mankind can awaken to the truth.

He made a tremendous demand. Towards the end of his life he sometimes wondered, very sadly and pitifully, whether he had not asked too much of his followers. I think, to mention only one particular, that he was wavering as to his ban upon tobacco. He was so certain of the happiness and joy which come from "salvation" that he had no patience with the trivial weaknesses of human flesh, which do not really matter. Let us remember that he had seen thousands of men and women all over the world literally transformed by his method from the most miserable animals into radiant and intelligent creatures conscious of immortality and filled with the spirit of unselfish devotion to humanity. Is it to be wondered at that the General of this enormous Army should scarcely doubt the wisdom of his first terms of service?

But towards the end he suffered greatly in his own personal life, and suffering loosens the rigidity of the mind. Those of his own household broke away from him, the dearest of his children died, trusted officers forsook him, some of those whose sins he had forgiven again and again deserted his flag and whispered scandal and tittle-tattle into the ears of degraded journalism. He was attacked, vilified, and denounced by the vilest of men in the vilest of manners. Sometimes, sitting alone by himself, blind and powerless, very battleworn and sad, this old man at the end of his life must have suffered in the solitude of his soul a grief almost intolerable. But he became more human and more lovable in these last years of distress.

We are apt to think that very remarkable men who have risen through opposition and difficulty to places of preeminence must sometimes look back upon the past and indulge themselves in feelings of self-congratulation. It is not often true. A well-known millionaire told me that the happiest moment in his life was that when he ran as a little boy bare-headed through the rain into his mother's cottage carrying to her in a tight-clenched fist his first week's wage – a sixpenny bit. Mr. Lloyd George told me he never looks back, never allows himself to dream of his romantic life. "I haven't time," he said; "the present is too obsessing, the fight is too hard and insistent." Mr. Chamberlain, in the early days of tariff reform, told me much the same thing. Perhaps we may say that men of action never look back. And so it was with General Booth. He might well have rested during these last few years in a large and grateful peace, counting his victories, measuring his achievements, and comparing the pulpit in Nottingham or the first wind-battered tent in East London with this innumerable Army of Salvation which all over the world has saved thousands of human beings from destruction.

Sometimes smaller men are able to save a family from disgrace, or to rescue a friend from some hideous calamity, or to make a crippled child happy for a week or two, and the feelings created by these actions are full of happiness and delight. But this old, rough-tongued, weather-beaten, and heart-tortured prophet, who had saved not tens but thousands, who could see with his own eyes in almost every country of the world thousands of little girls rescued from defamation, thousands of women rescued from the sink of horrid vice, thousands of men newborn from lives of unimaginable crime and iniquity, thousands of homes once dreary with squalor and savagery now happy and full of purest joy, nay, who could see, as I have seen in India, whole tribes of criminal races, numbering millions, and once the despair of the Indian Government, living happy, contented, and industrious lives under the flag of the Salvation Army – he who could see all this, and who could justly say, "But for me these things had never been," was not happy and was not satisfied. He ached and groaned to save all such as are sorrowful.

In the last letter he ever wrote to me, a letter that broke off pitifully, because of his blindness, from the big, bold, challenging handwriting, and became a dictated typewritten letter, occurred the words, "I am distressed." He was chiefly distressed by the over-devotion most of us pay to politics and philosophy, by the struggle for wages, by the clash between master and man, by the frivolity of the rich, the stupor of the poor, by the blindness of the whole world to the necessity for a cleansed heart. He did not want to establish a Salvation Army, but to save the whole world. He did not want to be acclaimed by many nations, but to see suffering and poverty and squalor clean banished from the earth. And he believed that with the power of the State at his back, and with the wealth now squandered in a hundred abortive directions in his hands, he could have given us a glad and unashamed England even in a few years. He knew this and he believed it with all his heart. And he held that his dictatorship would have hurt no just man. He suffered because poverty continues and thousands are still unhappy. For such men this world can never suffice. They create eternity.

Others may criticize him. And no man ever lived, I suppose, was easier for every little creature crawling about the earth in self-satisfied futility to criticize and ridicule. For myself, I can do nothing but admire, revere, honor, and love this extraordinary old realist, who saved so many thousands of human beings from utmost misery, who aroused all the churches of the Christian religion throughout the world, who communicated indirectly to politics a spirit of reality which every year grows more potent for social good, who was so tender and affectionate and cordial, and who felt for suffering and sorrow and unhappiness wherever he found it with a heart entirely selfless and absolutely pure.

Even if the Salvation Army disappeared from every land where it is now at work – and, though it will not disappear, I anticipate during the next ten years many changes in its organization – to the end of time the spirit of William Booth will be part of our religious progress. We cannot unthink ourselves out of his realism, out of his boundless pity, out of his consuming earnestness. He has taught us all to know that the very bad man can be changed into the very good man, and he has brought us back, albeit by a violent method, to the first simple and absolute principles of the only faith which purifies and exalts humanity.

When the dust has blown away, we shall see him as perhaps the greatest of our time.

General Booth's funeral cortege in downtown London, August 20, 1912

SOLDIER REST!
THY WARFARE O'ER

Philip Gibbs
The Graphic, (August 31, 1912)

Philip Gibbs (1877-1962), one of the best-known journalists of his day, wrote for The Daily Mail, Daily Express, *and* Daily Chronicle. *He also freelanced for various journals and magazines, and worked as a war correspondent on the Western Front from 1914-18. He knew almost every notable person in England, and wrote about most of them. Many of his experiences were turned into books, including* The Pageant of the Years: an Autobiography *and* Adventures in Journalism. *In the latter he relates an amusing anecdote: "I remember that at that time when I was working for Alfred Harmsworth at* The Daily Mail, *I had to see General Booth, the founder of the Salvation Army, that grand old man for whose humanity and love I had a great respect, in spite of his methods of conversion, with scarlet coats and tambourines. He was angry with something I had written, and was violent in his wrath. But then he forgave me and talked very gently and wisely of the responsibilities of journalism, 'the greatest power in the world for good or evil.' Presently the old man seized me by the wrist with his skinny old hand, and thrust me down on to my knees. 'Now let us pray for Alfred Harmsworth,' he said, and offered up a fervent prayer for his wisdom and light. I don't know what effect that prayer had on Harmsworth, but it seemed to have an immediate effect on my fate. I was 'sacked' from* The Daily Mail." *The piece offered here, so evident of Gibbs' affection for the General, was a eulogy, one of the finest, written at the moment of his death.*

The death of the General was the last victory in his long campaign. For when the world knew that the flame which had burned in that frail old figure had flickered out, when they learned that this old warrior – the chief of a great Army which has flung its outposts to the farthest corners of the world – had surrendered his sword to death, all his critics, all his scoffers, were silenced, and all we little men of life knew that a great one had passed away from us.

I saw him many times when his spirit was bright and burning. I watched him when he put his spell upon great multitudes of ordinary men and women, out of whose ordinariness he drew heroic and ideal qualities of courage and compassion and chivalry. I have seen that tall old man, whose eyes, even when they were almost sightless, burned with great spiritual fires of love and hate – a simple love for God and man, a simple hate for the devil and evil things – touch these people with the divinity of tears and laughter, and, by some magic, uplift them to great heights of enthusiasm and faith.

The mere sight of him, standing above them on a platform in some great hall, his white beard flowing over his General's coat, his eagle face peering down at them, his body swaying as the noise of their applause came up to him in gusts, was enough to stir his soldiers with an emotion which seemed to tear at their heartstrings. The sound of his voice, that hoarse whisper which used to reach one's ears from a far distance, seemed to strip off the rags and bindings and mummy clothes of the human soul and leave it naked and quivering before him. Brutal men, foul women, the dregs of life were caught by the throat, in the grip of his passion, so that in a little while he had them groaning and wailing at their beastliness and crying like little children for "salvation."

He used every art and trick of oratory, every crude and common method to "win souls to God." He would gibe and jest at them with a biting humor. He would use the slang of the slum, and the jargon of the thieves' alley. He would sing to them and dance to them, in a kind of religious ribaldry. He would make himself a buffoon for the love of God, and by these methods, and any methods, he would drag people up from the depths of misery, drag them by the scruff of the neck from the mire to cleanliness, give them back their manhood and their womanhood, and fan into a flaming torch the little spark of divinity which never goes out in the human heart, however deep it is in the abyss of degradation.

So I saw him in life, and a few days ago I saw him in death. In the Congress Hall at Clapton the old soldier lay at rest. The flags of his regiments, the trophies of his victories, were unfurled above his bier. The hymns which he had sung so often on the battlefield, in his hoarse quavering old voice, beating time with his thin, restless hands, with the joy of the melody in those wonderful eyes of his, were being sung now, softly and sweetly, above his coffin. And there he lay with the scent of flowers about him, his hands quiet and still, his eyes shut, but still with a little smile about his lips, and his grand old face beautiful in its peace and majesty. Close to him some of his officers stood on guard, as round the body of a dead king, holding his standards, motionless, with their heads bent, figures of grief. There was a woman "officer" among them, her face in shadow under a pokebonnet. It was the face of one of those women who at the General's bidding has gone into the darkest slums of modern cities, among the ugliest and most terrible things of life, bringing, with the rattle of a tambourine, and a cheerful smile, a message of love into lovelessness.

I watched part of the almost endless procession of men and women who came to this lying-in-state, and the memory of it will linger with me. This was a pilgrimage of people from the mean streets of the great city. Illustrious persons had sent wreaths and tributes, now and again a carriage stood outside the hall, but for the most part those who came to get one moment's glimpse of the old General's face were the children of poverty. Here were working men in their working clothes, and the women of humble life – those people who live always on a thin crust above the abyss, and who need great courage, great strength of character, great luck to prevent themselves from falling through. There were poor clerks, and down-at-heel fellows of shabby gentility, and out-of-works who have been into many an Army "shelter" on a winter's night, and poor devils who still look to the Army for something hot to drink, and something to ease the hunger pains. The instinct of loyalty, a genuine love for "the old man," a remembrance, perhaps, of some moment of rare emotion when their horny hands clutched up to God, had brought them, perhaps at the risk of losing a day's job, to his bier.

There was unrestrained emotionalism. Only by the quiver of a lip, by a moist eye, by a queer scared look on a rugged face, did one see that these people were moved profoundly. But it was a great and solemn sight, and men like myself, the lookers-on of life, the critics, the re-porters, who have not been followers of the General's flag, who follow, perhaps, other flags, or none at all, saw here the testimony to General Booth's greatness and the victory of his life. He had been the friend of humanity, the lover of those who had "gone under," and of all who suf-fer and sin. Now that he lay dead they did not forget.

The leaders of all churches, and people of all classes, even those who shrink from the peculiar methods of The Salvation Army, have joined in acknowledging the real grandeur of the old General and the influence of his work as an agency for uplifting and cleansing those who are most difficult to raise and purify. There are some who believe that with his death the spirit will depart from his worldwide organiza-tion. I am not one of those, for I believe that some at least of that ardent spirit shines through the ranks of his Army. There are many cheerful, devoted and enthusiastic souls among those who stand at the street cor-ners and follow the big drum. And the new General who has taken up his father's sword, humbly but bravely, is a man of unusual gifts, like most members of the Booth family, and with a far-seeing vision. The Salvation Army may change, but it will go on.

The mere sight of him seemed to tear at their heartstrings.

A TRUE GREAT HEART

William T. Stead
Fortnightly Review (Dec. 1912): 1042-50.

William Thomas Stead (1849-1912) was an English journalist and reformer. He was editor of the Darlington Northern Echo *when he first met The Salvation Army, complaining to William Booth that his "lasses" were overworked and undernourished. He later became editor of the* Pall Mall Gazette *(1883-1890) and again became involved with the Army when he solicited the help of Bramwell Booth in exposing London's "white-slave" trade in a series of articles called "The Maiden Tribute of Modern Babylon." For their action in "buying" Eliza Armstrong to prove their case, he and Bramwell Booth were prosecuted, with W.T. Stead serving six months in jail while Bramwell was discharged. In 1890 W.T. Stead founded London's* Review of Reviews, *which became a very prestigious journal and one in which he again actively promoted The Salvation Army. At about the same time he helped William Booth write* In Darkest England, and The Way Out *(published October, 1890). He was, therefore, quite well acquainted with the General, wrote a short biographical sketch of him in 1891, and, though William Booth was not always certain of his motives (and wary of his spiritualist beliefs), they seem to have had a strong attachment to each other. The personal tribute which follows was written shortly before W.T. Stead died in the* Titanic *disaster, April 1912. William Booth died in August of the same year.*

Who among living men is the most remarkable illustration of the immense potentiality latent in the human being to impress millions of his fellow men with a sense, first, of his existence, secondly, of his personality, and thirdly, of his ideas?

The question is one worthy of more than a moment's consideration. For, after all, the most important thing in the world is man, and the most important thing about man is the potential force that resides in his character. There are about fifteen hundred million human beings on this planet, fourteen hundred and ninety-nine million of whom are utterly unknown to all except the narrow circles of their families, their friends and neighbors. Of the remaining millions, how many are there who are known, even by name, outside their own country? Probably not more than fifteen hundred, if that many.

If we ask how many of these fifteen hundred have impressed any other nation but their own with a sense of their personality, or are exercising any appreciable influence outside their natural frontiers, we should reduce the number to one hundred and fifty at the most. Of these one hundred and fifty the first place may be given to sovereigns and presidents of great States whose position on the throne or on the presidential chair lifts them high enough above the heads of the dim common multitude for them to be the cynosure of every eye, but whose personality, with a few exceptions, such as Kaiser Wilhelm and Theodore Roosevelt, is seldom clearly enough defined to leave any definite picture on the retina of the human race. Which of us, for instance, can say what are the personal characteristics of the Mikado of Japan, the Emperor of China, or the Grand Lama of Tibet? It is not so much the man, as the occupant of a particular pedestal, whose name is familiar throughout the world.

The second place belongs to great statesmen, of whom, however, there are but few whose names are known in both hemispheres. The Pope of Rome occupies a place by himself by virtue of his office, but who knows even the name of the Greek Patriarch of Constantinople or the Procurator of the Holy Synod in Russia?

Great men of science and explorers, great artists, great actors and actresses and singers, all these may be included in the category without overcrowding the seats allotted for the one hundred and fifty men of whom the human race as a whole knows something. Great millionaires, railway builders, financiers are known by their wealth or by their works, but seldom as living human beings. In wartime great generals and great admirals undoubtedly impress their personality on the mind of mankind.

But in these times of peace, burdened only with preparations for wars which happily do not arrive, fighting men are not heard of much beyond the barrack room or the ship's mess.

It is evident, therefore, that there are very few men now alive who have any real personal existence to their fellow men. It is doubtful whether there be as many as a baker's dozen.

Among that baker's dozen General Booth stands easily first. He is the man who has been seen by the greatest number of human eyes, whose voice has been heard by the greatest number of human ears, and who has appealed to a greater number of human hearts, in a greater number of countries and continents, not only more than any man now alive, but – thanks to the facilities of modern travel – than any man who has ever lived upon this planet. That in itself is a unique distinction. But when we have to add to this that he has called into being devoted companies of men and women in fifty-four different countries and colonies, and that he has done all this without any advantage of wealth, station, patronage, or education, enough has been said to justify the claim that in many respects General Booth is the most remarkable man living.

We may dislike his theology – the worse we think of it, the more our wonder should increase that a man so handicapped should have done so much. We may criticize his methods, but the more faulty his tactics the more amazing the results which he has achieved. We may doubt the permanence of his work, but it has at least come into existence, and a man who builds even a mud hovel on solid earth is greater than he whose airy castles of the imagination ever materialize themselves into actual reality.

As an example of what one man can do, unaided save by his wife, in the face of overwhelming obstacles, the career of General Booth forms one of the most inspiring and encouraging stories of our times. For what man has done man can do. General Booth has widened our conception of the possible. He has strengthened our confidence in the infinite potentialities of the individual. And if only for that he deserves and has received the gratitude of mankind.

General Booth is now eighty-one years of age. He has lost the sight of one eye, and sees with difficulty with the other. But he is active and vigorous as if he were only twenty-five, and he is continually engaged in campaigns entailing more continuous effort in traveling and speaking than the exertions which once in four years are made by the most sought-after speakers in presidential campaigns. As a mere specimen of physical endurance, of vital energy, he is without a peer. This is all the more wonderful because he had not originally a strong constitution. When he was a young man a doctor to whom he went told him that physically he was entirely unfit to be a preacher, and that twelve months of it would land him in the grave. He has had sixty years of it, and the latest doctor's certificate guaranteed him as good for another ten years' work. Like St. Francis, he has been hard upon his body. But it has responded marvelously to the calls made upon it. Open-air speaking, as John Wesley discovered more than a hundred years ago, is a capital cure for many physical ailments.

General Booth, inordinate in labor, has ever been most temperate in food and drink. When a doctor advised him to take a little port wine for his infirmities, his future wife wrote to him to "flee the detestable thing as you would a serpent." He has been all his life an absolute abstainer. At one time in his history he made up for this by the copiousness of his libations of tea. "I have been saved from drink," he said to me once, "I have been saved from tobacco, but I have not been saved from tea." It is said that he rivaled even Dr. Johnson in the number of cups of tea which he would consume at a sitting. Of recent years he has been saved from the inordinate use of tea. I have not seen him exceed a cup or two for many years past.

In diet he is very abstemious: "take a little at a time and take it frequently," seems to be his rule, and as his years increased he has diminished his daily rations. Mr. Hereward Carrington has written a book in which he maintains that vitality has nothing to do with nutrition, and that food is not necessary to preserve life or maintain strength. By endorsing that paradox, there is no doubt that General Booth gets more foot-tons of energy out of a very spare diet than are generated in the frames of other men who consume four and five times as much food a day as the General.

The General has never been an athlete, nor have I ever heard of his practicing any other method of keeping his body in training than that of constant work and talk while he is awake, and of sound sleep when he is in bed. His physical form is frail, but put him on his feet before a large audience and the only difficulty is to stop the torrential flow of his speech. His mental faculties show no sign of decay. His spirit is as young as it was when he started the Salvation Army; his ambition even vaster, and his confidence in the future is as remarkable as the buoyancy of his spirit.

In estimating the extent, the depth, and the force of the influence of this man's personality, it should never be forgotten that he started life without the advantages which are the natural inheritance of the cultured class. His reading, although extensive in certain directions, has been singularly limited in others. I should doubt very much whether he has ever read the plays of Shakespeare. The classical literature of Greece and Rome has been to him a sealed book. You may search through his speeches in vain for any allusions to the sources which have been a perennial spring of inspiration to other men.

The Bible to him is all sufficient; not that he is a man of a single book, for, especially in his later years, he has been a voracious reader of books that promised to give him light upon the path which he was pursuing in the founding and organizing of The Salvation Army. But the immense stores of experience which have been acquired by the Church of Rome in its history of nearly two thousand years have not been utilized by him. The guidance of colleges, universities, or professors, the episcopal direction of bishops, or the stimulus that comes from belonging to a great teaching order, all these things have been denied him. He did his work very largely out of his own head with the assistance of his wife and his two great manuals, the Old and New Testament scriptures and the rules and regulations of the British Army.

The great secret of his success is to be found in the concentration of all the forces of a very strong personality upon the achievement of a great end. He was from his boyhood consumed by a passion for souls, a passion which extended itself in later years to a great desire for the welfare of their bodies, that is, on the human side. General Booth himself would maintain that all his enthusiasm for humanity would have profited him nothing had he not been sustained and directed by the constant practice of earnest prayer.

Nothing less like the ordinary conventional prayer than the petitions which The Salvation Army and its founder hurl, rather than address, to the Supreme Being can hardly be imagined. In their half-minute prayer meetings they carry the principle of repressing vain repetitions or the use of many words to its ultimate limit. At such meetings their prayers are almost telegraphic in their conciseness. They say what they want, say it with emphasis, then, having said it, they say "Amen" and have done with it.

Far be it from me to suggest that this is the only form of prayer which is favored by General Booth. It has been his habit of old to break out into audible vocal prayer in the midst of a conversation carried on either with a single companion or with a company of friends. When Cecil Rhodes came back from Hadley, the farm colony of the Army, General Booth was impelled to have a brief session of prayer in the railway carriage, a unique experience for Cecil Rhodes, but one which he remembered with profound respect. No one who has ever been present on such an occasion can resist the conviction that such a method of procedure is as natural as it is logical. To a company engaged in discussing things pertaining to the Kingdom – and in General Booth's thinking there are very few things that do not pertain to the Kingdom – there is ever present One Invisible from Whom spring all the good impulses of the human heart, and with Whom, therefore, it seems the most obvious thing in the world to converse reverently but frankly, asking for guidance and help in carrying out what the General believes to be His will.

Many a time have I been present at such scenes when at headquarters or in his house. After a long, heated argument the General will say, "It is time we prayed over this." Without more ado he would fall down and pour out his soul in strenuous supplication; a junior partner pleading, as it were, with the senior for direction, for consolation, and for strength to do His will. There is no insincerity about General Booth's piety. He is simplicity itself. His range of vision may be narrow, but it is very keen. He has firmly grasped two great ideas. The first is that an enormous number of human beings are not living the life which their Maker, or even any benevolent man, would wish them to lead; and secondly, that they could be brought much more into accordance with the ideal if they believed as he did, and fashioned their lives accordingly.

This, it may be said, is the belief of all religious teachers. But few religious teachers of the present day, at least, are so absolutely certain as General Booth, who does not have any doubts, has no room for doubts, that is to say within the sphere of action. Outside the sphere of action there is a wide area in which he will admit there is room for speculation and hesitation, but in the vital things relating to the welfare of the human family he is absolutely certain, first, that things are not as they ought to be; second, that they would be much better than they are if people believed as he did.

General Booth's creed is the old orthodox evangelical revivalist creed, but it is tempered by a very intense sympathy for the frailties of humanity and a statesmanlike grasp of the problems with which he has to deal. No one ever hears General Booth say a disrespectful word of any other system of religion; this is especially true of the Roman Church. There is, indeed, much more sympathy between General Booth and the Pope than between him and, let us say, the Archbishop of Canterbury. Between Cardinal Manning and the General there were innumerable points of sympathy. Both men had a profound respect for each other. Of the poor, toiling, hardworking Roman priest in the slums of our great cities, I have always heard General Booth speak in terms of enthusiastic admiration.

In his early youth he repudiated all narrow and exclusive doctrines which limited the range of divine grace. "I must preach a salvation," he declared, "as universal as the love of God." He contemplates the human race as a whole. He realizes intensely how very inadequate are the agencies which are working for the betterment of humanity, and although he may deplore what he considers erroneous in the teaching of many religions, he recognizes them all as allies insofar as they uplift man from the brute and lead him Godward. In this respect he is much more broadminded than his wife, who was more disposed to be militant and aggressive than her husband. She passed away twenty years ago. Had she been living to this day she might have gone through the same mellowing process which has produced such good results in her husband.

When King Edward died General Booth paid public testimony to the service which the late sovereign had rendered to the country, the peace of the world, and the Salvation Army. Of the three of them the General mentions the Salvation Army last, but probably in his mind he put it first, for being but mortal it cannot be wondered at that he should occasionally be disposed to overestimate the comparative importance of the work in his hands. He believes that he was the instrument of divine wisdom in creating the Salvation Army, and one detects an occasional tendency to assume that the Almighty has given the Salvation Army a special commission for the conversion of the world. It is a venial fault, and General Booth is saved from the worse forms of this absorption in his own organization by the constant consciousness of the immensity of the work which he cannot overtake.

With all his great qualities General Booth would have been lost had he not possessed the saving gift of humor. He is a merry man at heart, despite his somewhat somber view as to the present condition and future destinies of the human race. No one loves a good story better, no one, not even Mr. Bryan, tells a story better. He said to me one time with a twinkle in his eye: "If you only knew what expostulations I receive from some good folks because I make my audience laugh, but I cannot do without a little humor now and then." I have never heard him make a speech, no matter how earnest, no matter how deadly serious it may have been in the main, that was not lit up now and then by a ripple of laughter. Shakespeare found it necessary to alleviate the gloom of his tragedies by the humor of his clowns, and General Booth never seems to find any incongruity in passing from grave to gay, from lively to severe, and prefacing a solemn appeal to the terrors of the law by some familiar story from low life which sets his audience in a titter.

In politics the General has never taken part. If he had not been a religious man he would probably have been a socialist. When he was only thirteen years of age he said, "Chartists are for the poor, therefore I am for the Chartists." His sympathies are democratic and cosmopolitan. With Tom Paine, he would say that the world was his parish, and that to do good was his religion. One world, one race, one destiny would sum up his view of things.

He is absolutely colorblind as to race prejudice. I remember once he spoke to me somewhat slightingly about the colored race, and I showed by my reply that I had misunderstood him. He checked me at once: "When I speak of them I mean those poor creatures who black themselves over with burnt cork and perform antics as Christy Minstrels, not the colored citizens of the United States." This absence of all colored prejudice has stood him in good stead in his mission to India, Japan, and elsewhere. To him a man is primarily the casket of an immortal soul, and souls have no skins of any color.

He has a keen business sense. It required no small degree of financial genius to create an organization out of nothing, which commands an income at the present day of a million dollars – a feat which entitled him to the respect of the greatest geniuses of the world of finance. One of the most brilliant of his financial inspirations was the Self-Denial Week, which this year produced the sum of three hundred and fifty thousand dollars in Great Britain alone, raised for the most part in cents, by the simultaneous action of the whole organization concentrated for seven days upon the one idea of doing without something in order to contribute to the revenue of the Army.

Money comes to those who can use it, and no one can deny that the Salvation Army makes a good return for the funds entrusted to its stewardship. Lord Rosebery once said that he heartily wished the whole administration of the English Poor Law could be handed over to the Salvation Army. In many British colonies the government has begged the Army to take over the care of discharged prisoners, and various governments have found it sound economy to grant subsidies to the Army in consideration of its undertaking the performance of certain duties to the poor and the outcast, which the state found itself incapable of adequately performing.

Great as has been the success of General Booth, he would probably be the first to admit that, compared with what he had hoped to do, his work has been in many respects a magnificent failure. The same thing may be said about Christianity. It is nineteen hundred years since the Crucifixion, and one-half of the world is still outside the Christian pale. The General would like to have seen the Army made the instrument for the redistribution of population throughout the planet. To the utmost of the means placed at his disposal he has endeavored to develop colonization and to direct immigration. But the means at his disposal were miserably inadequate. Such a task can only be undertaken by an authority capable of drawing upon the whole resources of the nation by means of taxation. In this, however, as in other respects, he has been a pioneer. The work that he has done, still more the work which he has tried to do, will be an inspiration and encouragement to those who will come after him. Yet it seems absurd to speak of even comparative failure whenever we contemplate the actual achievements of this remarkable man.

In the days when General Booth was only the Reverend William Booth, ordained minister of the Methodist New Connexion, he was brought up short by the refusal of the conference of the Connexion to allow him to continue any longer the work of general evangelization. The conference solemnly voted, all protest notwithstanding, that the Reverend William Booth must conform to the regular rule of the denomination, and appointed him to be minister of the circuit.

Mrs. Booth, who was in the gallery when the division was taken, could not control her indignation. Rising from her seat, with flushed face and flashing eye, she bent over the gallery towards her husband and uttered the one word, "Never." Mr. Booth sprang to his feet, waved his hat, and rushed to the door. At the foot of the stairs he clasped his wife in his arms. The Rubicon was passed.

That was in 1861. They were thirty years of age and had a young family of four children. "We went out together," says General Booth, "not knowing whither we went. We didn't know a soul who would give us a shilling. We fell back on the home of one of our parents and then waited on God."

From such small beginnings – a penniless couple outcast from a minor Methodist sect – sprang the Salvation Army. Who could have foreseen that the outcome of that brave resolve would have been the creation of an organization whose members by a single week's self-denial could raise a sum of five hundred thousand dollars a year? No one, least of all General Booth. But in our own time, under the incredulous eyes of an unbelieving and materialistic generation, this miracle was performed.

His confidence in the future is as remarkable as his buoyancy.

A LEADER AND COMMANDER OF THE PEOPLE

Lady Frances Balfour
in *General Booth* (London: Nelson, 1912)

Frances Balfour (1858-1930) was the daughter of the Duke and Duchess of Argyll who married Eustace Balfour, brother of the Prime Minister of England. She was a staunch liberal and prominent member of the Liberal Women's Suffrage Society. She was, however, opposed to violence in her campaign for women's right to vote. After women won that right, she became a well-known writer, mainly of articles and biographies. Obviously an admirer of William Booth and The Salvation Army, she takes as the basis for her impressions her meeting with him (in the company of other dignitaries) at the thirty-ninth anniversary celebrations at the Crystal Palace in July 15, 1904. The day, part of the Third International Congress, was called "Thanksgiving Day," and saw more than 70,000 people make their way to the Crystal Palace in southeast London. Though obviously eulogistic and perhaps too superficial to portray the Founder's personality, her insights are consistent with most other impressions held by prominent people.

It was in the year 1904 that I had an opportunity of personally studying the General of that Army whose battle lines have been so far flung in this our day and generation.

We look upon the past pages of history and dream ourselves back in some of its chapters. The age of chivalry calls to some, or the days when the land had rest and the people were entering into their rights; or it may be the ages when the Reformation claimed its martyrs, or when liberty and the emancipation of the slave thrilled "the broad earth's aching breasts." Each epoch has its call to the spirit that flings itself backward over the ages. It is not always so easy to recognize the

97

prophets of our own time, to see where the story of today is tracing the record which will be the history of the future. There are men and women whom we dismiss with a phrase or brush by unheeding, who will, when the roll call is sounding through the past, be reckoned among life's chosen heroes. Then will our descendants ask if we knew what it was ours to live near; if we saw, or if our eyes were holden; did we show ourselves worthy or blind? So will they envy or condemn; and even as they judge us, their own feet may be caught in the same un-heeded snare.

There are many people living who can recall the time when they first heard of the Salvation Army; the shock its title gave to those who, how-ever often they have repeated the prayer for the Church militant here on earth, never conceived that an Army could be organized girded only with "the whole armor of God." They asked if these men with untutored voices, clad in red jerseys and blue coats, blowing trumpets and beat-ing drums, led by so-called officers, which included women with mili-tary titles, moving in companies beneath a red and yellow flag bearing the strange device, "Blood and Fire"– were these disturbers, preaching and praying in the streets and marketplaces, were they to be called Salvationists?

The Army came into being in an age when the churches were not dead. Culture, art, and science had all been the handmaids of religion. Could such overt ways and startling self-advertising further the cause of true religion?

Thirty-nine years ago men had to seek out the leader and com-mander of this new Army. They asked who and what was the General, and the few were able to answer that he was a Wesleyan minister who had filled his chapel with the poorest and most degraded of his brethren, and that when there was no room found for them, he had gone out and stood up in the open streets and byways, compelling men to lis-ten to his plan of campaign.

The General's eloquence must always have been of the homely or-der. He had the gift of a ready flow of good English; the marks of an obvious, sincere desire to deliver himself of a burden of thought and to put it plainly before his hearers; a practical, wise, shrewd insight into human character; a conviction, as he told his hearers on the thirty-ninth anniversary of the Army, that every individual possessed a heart, and the Salvation Army had sought ever to reach that citadel of life.

A Colonial governor observed, as he looked down from the Crystal Palace on those wide terraces thronged with that Army of trained soldiers of the cross: "The General is the only man who can command many millions, to tear the world in pieces, or to heal it." As the eye ranged over the ordered ranks, another saying of a great statesman came to the mind: "In the Middle Ages, William Booth would have founded a great monastic order." Who can say what such a natural leader of men might not have done with the forces he had called, chosen, and trained in the thirty-nine years of his mission, had his own life and purpose not been consecrated to the obedience of a disciple of the supreme authority which rules the hearts of men? The evidences of Christianity are more miraculously revealed in their controlling forces on individual ambitions than, perhaps, in any other way.

For General Booth's individuality was autocratic and dominant, with a manner bordering on the severe and dictatorial. To some of the guests on the occasion I speak of he was known in private. He had held counsel with them, as legal authorities, in the days when his Army often appeared in the police courts of the country. There were colonials, who had grasped his wide schemes of colonization and settlement, and who had given his officers the keys to their jails, knowing that their influence would help to keep them empty. There were financiers, who had given largely twenty years before, when the General parodied *Darkest Africa* with his story of *Darkest England,* and bade a whole country gaze on and consider its submerged tenth. The country never gave him the hundred thousand he commandeered, but as the pages of that book are turned in the light of a quarter of a century, therein is written plainly that Booth was the practical interpreter of the lonely prophet, Thomas Carlyle. The General knew quite well that his guests had not come to be "soundly saved," but to do honor to one who had raised himself to a great power. None of those who came in touch with him that day will ever forget the impression of the man. We had seen him in the nave, surrounded by his orchestral hosts, speaking, leading the music with impetuous gesture, bearing his seventy-nine years as a watch in the night.

We turned from the spectacle, from the stir of a great crowd, and we passed to where we were to meet him. We waited in the anteroom, and suddenly he was in our midst, a few staff officers around him. He moved with a swinging step, turning rapidly from side to side. The officers sought to make some special introductions, but he would not listen: "I ask them who they are, and that is shortest." The form was familiar – tall and thin, the narrow, eagle-nosed head, the sweeping beard, the haggard, spare, hard-bitten look. What arrested attention were the eyes, a hazel-green color, with small pupils. The glance was as restless as the personality, but as he shook hands, with a clinging grip without much pressure, there was a flash of instantaneous recognition, a human, concentrated consciousness. The first thought was that of a prophet of the erratic, impulsive type; another impression, not at first altogether agreeable –was that of a man conscious of power, and not disdaining dramatic effects.

The power and authority made us rise as before a great conqueror; the self-consciousness gave us a sense of disappointment. Perhaps the Napoleonic pose comes to every man who is self-made and has raised himself by his own genius for command over his fellows, and rules by the power that is born in him. Rule was the word. Every movement was autocratic and domineering. The staff came and went around him, with orders or with care for his own well-being. Their manner had a military subordination, tempered by a humble affection; but no man seemed to approach him in perfect confidence. It was possible to believe that the hasty speech of a naturally impatient temperament might at times be shown. His words to them were short and decisive, but not rough. Not till later did we see the love that has no fear. One of his grandchildren entered a room where he was talking alone with a few who remained after the guests had departed. The child came behind him, and placing a hand on each side of his face, bent over and kissed him on the lips. He took no notice, and when released, continued his absorbed conversation.

After moving among the guests, the General bade us pass into the room where tea was ready, and he addressed us from his place. There was no formality about his speaking. He knew his subject as he knew his own life. That it was not threadbare was due to the vitality, humor, and fire of his delivery. There we were, he said, and we had better get to business at once, and he would begin by asking a blessing on the meal – which he did in very simple and rather hasty words. Tea over, the officers told us that the General would speak to us. We ranged ourselves, about fifty or sixty, among the tables, facing him. The General stood opposite that long glass side of the room. The heat of the summer day was tempered by a drifting, fine rain, which obscured the wide horizon to "gray Surrey fading into blue." His eyes, as he spoke, seemed fixed in space; but as the words poured themselves forth, the audience could feel that the arrows of his argument, sarcastic, humorous, and pointed, were winged with a consummate knowledge of the human nature waiting for his words.

The voice was broken and weak, worn as an instrument which had been used to its fullest capacity. Beneath, on the terrace, were the bands, moving to take up their places, as the Army prepared for its march past. The officers, fearing we should not hear the General, began to close the windows. Half were shut, when, peremptorily and with some excitement, he bade them stop. "Don't suffocate them till the collection is taken." Throughout, the speech was addressed to the class he knew was before him. It was the year when Port Arthur had fallen, and when the fiscal controversy was at its bitterest. We had seen him quench the storm of applause which had greeted the Japanese contingent by saying that the Army knew no blood and fire but in its power to save. He told us he had looked over the ranks gathered in the Palace. Whence came this obvious cheerful devotion of that multitude, a mass redeemed from the depths of sin and degradation, and leading lives so religious they might be bishops? "This is my fiscal reform," – as he spoke of his new plans how to reach and touch the human heart hidden in the most degraded. "All here are beautiful, all love work, and are workers."

We could not tell whether he spoke out of an abounding charity or because he felt we were worth girding into action. He never seriously touched on politics, never reviewed the past, or reminded us of the hostility and coldness the Army met with in its early days. "I stood up alone, without knowing where to turn for a shilling, and there gathered round me the brains and hearts that planned then, and still spend their time planning for the good of the Army." There were allusions which made us understand he knew our weakness and our critical attitude. It was done in a flashing, good-humored note: we were there that he might use and not abuse us.

One was there who told us that the King had asked the General, "Do the parsons help you?" and he had replied, after a minute's hesitation, "They imitate me." The strength of the General's position has always been that he has ignored criticism; and, sure of his own position, he has led public opinion and never heeded or given criticism. The Army has hewn its own path amid the dark forests of vice and ignorance, and has relied on its leader alone; their watchword, love; their doctrine, works. For an organization which has its roots in Christianity its outlets are material and intensely utilitarian. It was the waste of human energy and life which appealed to the General, the wretchedness of the surroundings of those who had gone under.

From the first he declared it was no use preaching salvation to the famished, the diseased, and those whose bodily needs claimed their whole minds. "We take them, we wash them, we dress them, we bless them." The spiritual impetus must have been largely supplied by that remarkable woman who was the comrade in arms and in love of the General. Those who heard Mrs. Booth speak in the power of her deep spiritual convictions, who saw radiating from her the gifts that Christ gave to His disciples, and which in the world's history seem so often to have been bestowed upon women, understood the deep inspiration which she was to the practical, organizing mind of the founder of the Army of Salvation.

There are certain individuals who never seem quite of this earth, earthly. They seem visitants from a world whose light still shines on their faces; their feet seem but lately to have trodden the streets of a city celestial. There are others, again, whose influence seems to be that of idealizing the things that are seen and which are material. Nothing is hidden from their eyes. Their imagination penetrates the darkest ways, and seeing, they also believe they know the road which leads to a higher, more humane, more Godlike state of things. They dwell in the Interpreter's House, and to this order General Booth belonged. He understood the evil he wished to fight, and he forged his own weapons and levied his own forces. He saw the vice, ignorance, and misery of a section of the community; he determined he would use the qualities of the same class to raise and redeem their brethren.

The work demanded of his Army was of the severest physical nature. He chose his officers from the ranks of the toilers. He asked of them faith in their Divine Master, in His power to save. He demanded that they should have a conviction that their own hearts were steadfastly set on salvation. To himself he enforced an obedience as great as ever exacted by the General of the Order of Jesus. No officer was obliged to remain a day in the Army, but while they wore the uniform their obedience was to be complete. "A telegram from me may send them to any part of the world, and they must go." By his side or in remote regions they were trained to set the highest example of self-denial and of toil. But in his genius he did not forget the human nature of his officers. They were bound by no vows which kept them from the solace of family life, which deprived them of the love of children. Trained to obedience, they were granted a large discretion, and while their leader lived his long career, the Army was never divided by disruptive self-seeking.

After the speaking we were to see him receive that countless multitude, representing forty-nine nations and tongues, as they passed him in review order. Each nation was headed by its own band, wore its distinctive dress, bore the banners of its nation, as well as that of Salvation. The General returned after he had passed among them in his motor car, and standing amid his officers and visitors, he looked down on the moving mass which still acclaimed him. He seemed almost unmoved, and again there came into his eyes the vision that seemed aloof and beyond the objects around him. After a time he sat facing the window in an armchair, and he talked long and earnestly to Lord Grey. He spoke low and rapidly, constantly moving a walking stick in his hand. Sometimes he held it across his forehead, or tapped the ground with it. The figure was never for an instant in repose, neither were the long, mobile fingers. He appeared absorbed in his visitor, and oblivious of all besides. Once his officers told him that the foreigners, all massed under one banner and captain, were passing. "Look, sir, at the foreign corps." He passed again unto the balcony. He explained their nationalities, while they looked up and sang some national hymns. He waved to them, but still with the air of detachment. It was possible to realize how he flung his regiments on the works of the great enemy, believing their lives of little moment if they could but rescue those his vision knew to be worth losing lives to save. So have the greatest commanders looked over the armies they have used for the kingdoms of this world. . . .

The closing scenes consisted of the combined music of the massed bands; and amid that sea of trumpets and the voice of praise of a great host we were to see close the day which had brought us into personal touch with a General who was looking back on thirty-nine years, and who knew that this great Army must soon be led by another leader.

At the tomb of Lazarus in Bethany, outside Jerusalem

REVIVAL THEOLOGY

Harold Begbie

The Life of General William Booth
(London: Macmillan,1926); Vol. I: 257-260.

Harold Begbie (1874-1929), who wrote what still stands as the best biography of William Booth (published variously between 1919 and 1926), had ample opportunity to study the General's character, for he got to know him well when writing his several books featuring the Army: Broken Earthenware (1910), In the Hands of the Potter (1911) *and* Other Sheep (1911). *He also had a better opportunity than any writer since to examine William Booth's personal papers (letters, diaries) when he wrote his biography, for much of that material was destroyed when the International Headquarters was bombed and burned during World War II. One of the great pleasures of reading his biography is his frequent, often speculative, personal accounts of William Booth's character traits, especially regarding his success as a preacher and leader. In the following account of the General's "crude" theology, he proves a very perceptive and astute judge of character, and his analysis stands as one of the best of its kind.*

The revivalism of William Booth proceeded from the depths of his own soul as well as from his theological convictions. He was a man sharply conscious of his own faults, plagued by temptations of body and mind, the unhappy victim of morbid infirmity. So far as the current theology confirmed his settled opinion that every ill wish which visited his mind came from Satan, the adversary of souls, so far as theology influenced his conduct. But it was really this presence in himself, this continual companionship, of a nature inferior to that higher nature of which he was conscious in moods of religious exaltation; the perpetual haunting, the unlifting pressure of an evil spirit antagonistic to his peace; the breath on his cheek, the whisper in his ear, the guidance at his elbow, the flame and fire perpetually within his blood of a demon plotting the eternal ruin of his soul – it was this root of evil in himself, and not theology, which drove him first upon his knees and then into the streets as a preacher of salvation.

Nothing was more certain to him than the existence of Satan – the proof thereof tortured his own heart. So evil did he feel himself to be that his thought was not in the least staggered by the punishment of eternal hell. So profoundly conscious was he in moments of religious peace of a relief from this inner torment that he could believe that it came only from the mercy of God, a gift of the Son who had died to save his soul from death. Thus, so far as theology confirmed his experience, he was a theologian; but it was out of his own travail of soul that he fashioned his religion; and religion for him, from first to last, was a matter of the most personal piercing experience. He feared and hated the devil; he adored the Son of God, who had given him the victory over sin. Saturated through and through, penetrated and interpenetrated by this sense of an overwhelming gratitude to Christ; conscious, also, in himself of the most pervasive and sufficing happiness in his union with God, what could he do but go to those in darkness and ignorance, proclaiming with a vociferation, never mind how loud and alarming, the good news of a free and perfect salvation?

In an account he has given us of one of his earliest sermons – that under which the daughter of his tutor, Dr. Cooke, was converted – we see with perfect clearness the simple character of his theology at this time – he was then 22 – and also the driving force of personal experience at the back of his preaching:

> I described a wreck on the ocean, with the affrighted people clinging to the masts between life and death, waving a flag of distress to those on shore, and, in response, the lifeboat going off to the rescue. . . . I reminded my hearers that they had suffered shipwreck on the ocean of time through their sins and rebellion; that they were sinking down to destruction, but that if they would only hoist the signal of distress Jesus Christ would send off the lifeboat to their rescue. Then, jumping on the seat at the

back of the pulpit, I waved my handkerchief round and round my
head to represent the signal of distress I wanted them to hoist.

One's first instinct is to shudder. Without being supercilious or hy-
persensitive one may justly shrink from the contemplation of this violent preacher with his waving handkerchief. But to be perfectly just,
one must ask whether the current theology, the theology everywhere accepted, proclaimed, and even used as a menace to mankind, did not vin-
dicate that leap to the seat at the back of the pulpit, did not justify the
waving of that pocket handkerchief around the preacher's head? Is it
true that millions of souls are shipwrecked, are sinking down to destruction – *everlasting destruction?* Is it true that they have only to cry
to the Savior of the world to be lifted out of the dark waters? Most important of all, is it true that unless they do call for mercy and forgiveness, the undying worm and the unquenchable flame will feed upon
their tortured souls forevermore? If this be so, if this is indeed the
teaching of the Church, can any method be indecorous, any tone too
strident, any gesture too violent, any antic too shocking and startling,
that rouses even one perishing soul to escape a calamity so unthinkable
as remorse and agony prolonged throughout the ages of eternity?
Again, one must in fairness contend that the perfectly polite and unruf-
fled seemliness of the orthodox, who cherish this theology as the truth
of God, is a matter not only indefensible to casuistry but repellent to the
most primitive instincts of humanity.

This sermon of the waving handkerchief is important because it
helps one to understand the crude theology of William Booth at the beginning of his career, and to see how real was the experience from
which he drew this violent illustration. He clearly held that every soul
born into human life was in peril of everlasting destruction; he believed
that every living soul, by its sins and rebellion, merited destruction; that
destruction must infallibly be its lot but for the atonement of Christ;
and there his theology ended and his humanity began. No intellectual test was asked, no adherence was demanded to a string of self-
contradicting formula; all that was needed even of the very worst was a
cry from the heart of their own helplessness for the mercy and forgiveness of an infinite Christ.

But there was something more; he tested the reality of that cry. He did not tell these troubled and affrighted souls that they had only to give up their sins, join a church, and go regularly to the public worship of God in order to be certain of an angel's destiny in Paradise; he told them that they must be born again; that they themselves at the very center of their being must suffer a will change so utter, a transformation so complete, a conversion so unerring, that the very face of life should appear to them forevermore altered and transfigured. The cry was their part – and they could do no more than cry; the change was the miracle of God. If their cry came very truly from the grief of a broken heart, from the bitter knowledge that of themselves they could do nothing to save themselves from judgment and destruction; then, of a surety, the miracle would descend swiftly to their relief. From the very first he preached this essential need of conversion, and never once did he make the forgiveness of God to depend either upon the easiness of a life of repentance or the difficulty of a theological proposition. He made it hard for the sinner, but only hard for his heart where it was a greater hardness that alone stood in the way of divine mercy.

This theology of William Booth was not greatly modified by experience; in later life, with a knowledge of the human heart probably unrivaled, he saw the same teaching of this old theology with an infinitely wider vision; but it must be confessed that he remained to the very end of his days a most intractable Philistine as regards the entire region of the intellect. What was merely a loose intuition in this respect during youth became in age a settled conviction. He detested the arrogance of dogmatic science. In the impatience of his sorrow for the oppressed he considered literature and the fine arts as mere playthings of a childish humanity. He turned his back on philosophy, as being often a trick of the devil to catch mankind with the delusions of the reason. He was born a provincial, and he remained a provincial. He must always be judged as a man who, for the sake of Christ, denied his period and lived without enthusiasm for human inquiry.

When we consider these things, remembering at the same time that he held the generally accepted theology of his day, we shall more easily sympathize with the spirit of his revivalism. He knew little or nothing of textual criticism, nothing of historical criticism, nothing of

German theology; nothing of psychology, nothing of philosophy, nothing of physical science. He knew nothing of architecture, nothing of painting, and nothing of classical music. Furthermore, at this period of his career he knew very little indeed of life; was acquainted, indeed, only with the dissenting aspect of the commonwealth, was in touch only with the outermost suburbs of human society. When he married Catherine Mumford he was an ill-educated pastor of a section of the Methodist body, a man only remarkable for his intensity of feelings, the honesty of his nature, and the power of oratory. But the reader of his letters must already have perceived that while he was this, and while on the surface he was nothing more, there was in the depths of this rough, willful, untutored being a gnawing hunger and a consuming thirst for sanctification, a great struggle for spiritual perfection, and a dogged, obstinate, unconquerable passion to do the will of God against the obstruction of hell itself.

Again and again throughout his letters there is the same foreshadowing of an ultimate immortality that exists, calmly and quietly, in the most perfect and imperishable of Shakespeare's sonnets – a cry, as it were, from the dark blackness of a soul overshadowed by the powers of evil and wretched with poverty, ignorance, and a will pulling contrary to the divine, a cry that somewhere, somehow, and sometime he will veritably strike an immortal blow for God and his fellow man. It is this conviction of a destiny, this heroic faith in a high calling on the part of a man hampered by physical weakness and hindered on every hand by authority and indifference, which most interests us in William Booth as a revivalist, helping us to maintain our sympathy, and to expect a greater man. First to his youthful friends in Nottingham, and afterwards with a much greater intensity and far more persistent reiteration to Catherine Mumford, he confided this feeling within himself of a power to do something for the salvation of man which should add fresh glory to religion. His friends believed in him, and Catherine Mumford, warning him against ambition, believed in him too. After long years of wandering in the wilderness, he was to enter the promised land and justify this faith in his destiny.

He was a man sharply conscious of his own faults.

A LADY LODGER'S ACCOUNT
OF THE BOOTH'S
HOME LIFE

Harold Begbie
The Life of General William Booth
(London: Macmillan, 1926), Vol I: 315-34.

When Harold Begbie wrote his monumental Life of General William Booth *(published in various editions between 1919 and 1926), he could rely not only on the voluminous private correspondence and diaries of the primary partici-pants, but could also interview people who had known the Booths well and who were still alive. One of these, whose memory was quite remarkable in its detail and vividness, was a Miss Jane Short. She had been converted under the ministry of Mrs. Booth and, along with Miss Billups, went to stay with the Booths in 1867 as a "paying guest." Begbie's redaction of Miss Short's de-scriptions of the Booth household and, in particular, of William Booth's per-sonal habits, are surprisingly intimate and immensely interesting.*

I t is not until the Booths take up their residence in Hackney – where their daughter Eva was born – that we are able to see them with any degree of clearness in the intimacy of domestic life.

One of the ladies who went to lodge with them in 1867 was Miss Jane Short, whose age sits lightly upon her, whose memory is as per-fect as the most exacting biographer could wish, and who is happily of a humorous disposition, with no desire in the world to exaggerate the remarkable qualities of her dead friends. Very often as she speaks of the Booth household she breaks into cheerful laughter, recognizing as shrewdly as any practical and unimaginative person the eccentricity of that family life. At the same time, her testimony is emphatic to the nobility of the Booths, and to the reality of their passionate religious zeal.

"To tell you the truth," she informed me at our first meeting, "I was terribly afraid of going to live with these dear folk, because I had been so often disappointed, grievously disappointed, in religious people. It seemed to me that the Booths could not possibly be in their home life what they were in their preaching. I thought I should see things and hear things which would distress me; I could not imagine it was possible for them to live their ideals. You see, I loved them so well that I quite shrank from finding my hero worship an illusion."

She had first encountered Mrs. Booth at Margate, where the latter was conducting a Mission, and afterwards had attended some of the preachings in the East End of London. Admiration of Mrs. Booth had quickly ripened into friendship, and William Booth had won her liveliest sympathy and her utmost enthusiasm at their first encounter.

"People who say that Mrs. Booth was the greater of the two," declares Miss Short, "do not know what they are talking about. Mrs. Booth was a very able woman, a very persuasive speaker, and a wonderful manager; but the General was a *force* – he dominated everything. I've never met anyone who could compare with him for strength of character. You knew the difference in the house directly he opened the door. You felt his presence in every department of the home life. He was a real master.

"You could never say No to the General!" she laughs. "It was he who decided, not I, that I was to live with them. When he said a thing had to be done, it was done, and quickly, too. We used to call him 'The General' long before there was any Salvation Army. He couldn't bear beating about the bush. Prevarication, like stupidity, exasperated him. Everything had to go like clockwork, but very much faster than time. I always say that he got forty-eight hours' work out of the twenty-four."

And, then, laughing quietly to herself, she says, "Of course he was odd. He often used to say to me, 'Sister Jane, the Booths are a queer lot,' and laugh mischievously, for he was often laughing. I've known him suddenly kneel down in the middle of breakfast and give thanks to God because a letter he had opened contained money for the Mission. He'd be tremendously in earnest one moment, and the next he'd be laughing at himself, saying that he was an odd fellow. He'd change, too, in a twinkling of an eye from gloom and dejection to a contagious hilarity that carried everything before it. He suffered in those days – neuralgia and indigestion; it was often dreadful to see how the poor man suffered; but he would fling it all off directly there was work to do, or if he had to comfort anybody else, particularly Mrs. Booth. His love for his wife was the most beautiful thing I have ever known. It really was an exquisite thing. You know, perhaps, that Mrs. Booth was a great invalid. Her sufferings, at times, made her irritable and exacting. The least noise on some occasions would almost distract her. Well, it was at such times as these that the love of the General shone out most beautifully. Never once did he say a harsh word, never once did he try rallying her with rough encouragement; no, he would be more courteous and chivalrous than ever; he would love her as tenderly and sweetly as if she were his sweetheart; and he would wait upon her, soothe her, and nurse with a devotion that I have never seen equaled. I don't mean that he himself was never cross or irritable. He was sometimes, in my opinion, a little too stern with the children. But his love for his wife, well, that was quite perfect; and when I look back now I can see very clearly that it was this wonderful and beautiful love for Mrs. Booth which made the greatest impression on my mind. I may forget other things about them, but I shall never forget the General's love for his wife."

The house in which they lived, No. 3 Gore Road, Hackney, was one of those detached, double-fronted, family residences which are typical of the London suburbs and therefore characteristic of the English bourgeoisie. With a half-basement, a steep flight of steps to the front door, large plate-glass windows, and a complete carelessness as to architectural style, this big house had every impressive charm which appeals to the middle-class English family. It looked a rich man's dwelling; it was separate from its neighbors; it possessed large living rooms; and the road in which it lifted up its solid virtues was reputable and uneventful to the point of monotony. It was what people call the house of a substantial man.

The other lodger was Miss Billups, daughter of the rich contractor at Cardiff who had already befriended the Booths' Mission out of a lively gratitude for spiritual blessings. This lady was a trifle exacting, and never perhaps became quite a member of the family. But Miss Short, who was soon known affectionately as Sister Jane, not only, on occasion, shared her bedroom with one of the children, and became a very intimate and beloved member of the family, but worked herself nearly to death's door in the service of the Mission.

Although the demands of the Mission were enough to disorganize the best-regulated family in the land, there was a steady sense of orderliness in this household. Meals, for instance, were served to the moment, and woe betide the child who came in five minutes late. The General never sat at the head of his table when Mrs. Booth was present, but always beside her. She carved a dinner, or poured out the tea. The meals were of an extreme simplicity, and a generous rice pudding appeared on the table with every dinner – haunting the minds of the children to this day. Mrs. Booth held that no child need leave the table hungry, however meager the meal, so long as this rice pudding completed the feast. There were currants in it on special occasions.

Another characteristic of the Booth household was its tidiness. The General hated above everything else, except sin, untidiness, and dirt in every shape and form. His own study was a model of neatness. But he insisted that the same neatness should be observed elsewhere. The chairs were drilled like soldiers. Nothing was allowed to be out of place. The hearth must be swept continually. Books and toys were never permitted to be "left about."

One of William Booth's good qualities was a meticulous attention to personal cleanliness. Long before the bath was common in English life, he bathed himself every morning in cold water, with a hot bath once a week, and made use of a footbath two and three times during the week. He was very scrupulous in the matter of body linen, and though his things might be darned in every direction, they had to be extremely clean. He always wore long woolen stockings reaching above the knee, with old-fashioned garters wound around and around, and he never changed these articles without turning them carefully inside out; in his extreme old age, when he had to be waited upon, he would sometimes blaze into momentary ferocity if his attendant was slovenly. He was very often shabby, except in the matter of boots, but never slovenly. It is not difficult to see how the sympathies of such a man, to whom dirt was horrible and an evil smell so execrable that it often produced in him a fit of nausea, must have been quickened by the frightful barbarism of the London slums.

It seems to have been essential with him, even from the very beginnings of the Mission in London, that he should break away every now and then and get into the pure air and beautiful surroundings of the country.

"We used to make excursions into the forest," Miss Short told me, "and those were certainly among the General's happiest days. He was like a schoolboy as soon as he got away from London, laughing, singing, and joking nearly all the time. But, mind you, he never went away without his Bible in his pocket, and I think he hardly ever passed by a gypsy without speaking to him about his soul. I've heard him say to a man, for instance, cutting short a tale of some kind, 'But what you said was untrue. It was a lie. You ought not to tell lies. Don't you know it's wrong to tell a lie? What does God think of you when you say what isn't true?' And very well I remember that one day we were sitting at the foot of a great tree in the forest, he with his head on his wife's knee reading the thirty-sixth chapter of Ezekiel, when he suddenly raised his head at the words, *Then will I sprinkle clean water upon you and ye shall be clean; from all your filthiness, and from all your idols, will I cleanse you* – and fixed his eyes upon me, hard and shining, and demanded, 'Do you believe that, Jane Short?' – do you believe it – cleansed from *all* your filthiness?' I remember how that question seemed to flash into the depths of my soul."

This story reminded Miss Short of the General's curtness in religious discussions and in religious meetings. "He was always practical," she said, "and he detested insincere piety. If anybody prayed too long in a meeting, the General would cut him short with a loud 'Amen.' After a particular prayer meeting, which I very well remember for its marvelous influence upon many souls, the General sprang up and said: 'We've been in heaven; now for the work.' But insincere piety moved him to fierce anger, even the very semblance of it. A missionary came to him once in those early days and offered his services. The General inquired about his means of existence, and the man replied that he trusted in the Lord. 'Do you trust me, though?' demanded the General;

'come now, speak out; what do you want?' He was a wonderful, very nearly infallible judge of character; but he was taken in more than once – always, however, by men he had rather questioned from the first."

It may be imagined that a woman so delicate and so constantly engaged as Mrs. Booth had little time for the society of her children. She cut out and made most of their clothes; she heard their prayers, and for some reason she always insisted upon washing their heads; but neither her health nor her engagements, nor perhaps her disposition, allowed her to play with them. Miss Short considers them the most attractive children that ever breathed, declaring that the two chief impressions left upon her mind from those years, are first the wonderful love of William Booth for his wife, and, second, the delightful nature of the children.

"Of course they were odd," she says, smiling, "for, as the General told me, all the Booths are odd; but they were the frankest, purest, sweetest-minded children I ever knew. And the General knew this well, and although he was sterner than most parents are now, and certainly he did often whip where another would have tried gentler methods, still he loved them dearly, particularly Bramwell, who probably came in for more whippings than any of his brothers! And this is quite certain, the children adored their parents. They thought there were no two people in the world who could compare with their father and mother. The favorite game of the little girls in the nursery was a prayer meeting, and they used to have a penitent bench where the dolls were made to kneel. Often I have hardly been able to keep from laughing at the sight of a very ragged doll, all the hair gone and a great hole in the head, kneeling at the penitent bench. Bramwell was the first to show any inclination to depart from the lives of his parents. He wanted to be a surgeon; he would spend hours dissecting the body of a mouse. I remember that he once borrowed a doll from his sister Emma, and cut it open. She burst out crying when she saw the sawdust streaming away from it, and Bramwell exclaimed indignantly, 'Silly child! Do you think you can have an operation without blood?'

"But religion was the chief characteristic of the children's lives. I can tell you a story which shows how religion entered into their thoughts. My father, who lived a little distance from the Booths, was a very old-fashioned man, who smoked a church warden pipe and drank the usual drink of that day, gin and water. One afternoon Ballington Booth paid him a visit, and when my father's back was turned the naughty boy drank up a good deal of the gin and water! Directly he got home, he burst open the door of the room where his father was working, and exclaimed in quite a frenzy of alarm, 'Papa, Papa, I've broken my pledge!' It was some time before his agitation could be dispersed. I remember another story, too. When the same child had been naughty, his father said to him: 'Now would you rather that I prayed with you or whipped you?' Of course the child chose the prayer. Then the General said, 'We'll see what prayer will do for you; we'll try that first; if it doesn't make you a good boy I shall whip you.' It might not have been a wise thing to say, but the child was sincere, and really did pray to be a good boy."

Mrs. Booth was often unable at this time to bear the noise of the children, and they never played downstairs when she had retired. But William made it a rule, so far as his engagements would allow, to give them a part of his evenings at home, and the children would come charging into the room for a romp with their father. There was no set game, so far as I can discover, although "Fox and Geese" was a favorite, but a scrimmage of some kind was the usual amusement. William would lie full length upon the floor, and the smaller had to try and pull him up. He loved to be tousled; like other men of whom we have heard, he delighted in having his hair ruffled and his head scratched; he would sit reading a book with complete absorption, while one of his children sat upon the arm of his chair rubbing his head.

"One evening," says Miss Jane Short, "his daughter Emma, then about six, amused herself by putting his long hair into curl papers. She worked away until the whole head of the General was covered with little twists of paper – such a sight you never saw in your life. And when she had finished her work, the door opened and a servant entered announcing a visitor. Up sprang the General, and was all but in the hall when the children flung themselves upon his coattails and dragged him back, screaming with laughter. You can fancy that when the General looked in the glass he laughed too.

"By the way, I always think it is a good test of a man's character to know what his servants think of him; and certainly the servants in Gore

Road loved, I was going to say idolized, the Booths. The General might be harsh and abrupt at times, but they could not do enough for him, and they were never in the least afraid of him. I remember that sometimes, after a very exhausting Sunday, the Booths would take their breakfast in bed, and the maid used to laugh quite frankly at the General's appearance on these occasions. They felt for him every possible respect; but there was no fear and no severity in their attitude; they considered themselves members of the family, associated themselves with its fortunes, and entered as heartily into the religious enthusiasm of the household as into the fun and cheerfulness."

Although William had an almost unreasonable contempt for games – hating cricket and football as if they were sins – he entered with a boy's sympathy into the enthusiasm of his sons for animals. The garden at Gore Road was given up to rabbits, guinea pigs, rats, mice, and fowls. The boys owned these creatures and ruled over them, but the father drew almost as much pleasure from them as did the sons. He would go round the cages and watch the feeding. If a man of one idea, and that idea a burning consciousness of the existence of a God, can be said to have a hobby, the hobby of William Booth was this boyish delight in the pets of a back garden. His sons consulted him in every new venture, and he seems to have shared their excitement at every fresh addition to the menagerie. Bramwell Booth remembers that his father took a particular interest in his silkworms.

"I don't think any father could have been prouder of his children than the General," says Miss Short. "I am quite certain that it hurt him not to dress them up in beautiful clothes. But he insisted on simple, plain, strong clothes, not only for the sake of economy, but for the sake of setting an example. It used to make him furious when he saw the way in which poor people wasted precious money on stupid finery. He wouldn't even allow the family to go into mourning when Mrs. Mumford died, saying that the London poor ruined themselves by wearing black for a funeral. But he longed, I know, to see his children finely dressed, all the same. I've heard him say to them, 'When I get you all to heaven, I'll deck you; it will be safe there.' And once or twice he succumbed to temptation. I said to Mrs. Booth once, 'Wouldn't Herbert look lovely in a black velveteen suit with red stockings?' – and then I told him that it was shameful to dress such a beautiful child in plain, ugly things, asking him whether the poor would be any worse off for seeing the little child in velveteen. Well, I got my way for once; but the child only wore the suit two or three times. I think they carried this idea too far."

Another disastrous experiment in fine raiment carried with it a religious commentary. Mrs. Booth bought some beautiful silk for the girls' dresses, and gave it to one of the women converted in the Mission for making up, the material being too splendid for home manufacture. Unfortunately the temptation of this silk was too much for the Whitechapel woman, who disappeared with the material and was never heard of again. Mrs. Booth regarded this disaster as a lesson.

On one occasion some very fine toys were sent by rich people for a bazaar which Mrs. Booth was organizing in East London. Miss Short suggested that the children of poor people would not know what to make of such things, and counseled Mrs. Booth to buy them for her own children. "But she wouldn't listen to me," says Miss Short, "though I could see that she would have been pleased to possess the toys for her own children. She said they were intended for the poor, and the poor must have them; and she said that she had no right to spend money on such things. I never knew people in my whole life who had such a perfect horror of debt. There were times when they were exceedingly poor, driven, one might say, for a sixpence; but never once did they incur a single debt. Mrs. Booth told me that she would far rather starve than owe a penny, and the General held the same view. They were terribly strict where money was concerned."

With such views on clothes it may be guessed that the Booths entertained very strict notions as to the wearing of jewelry. What was their horror, then when Ballington walked into the room one day with a ring on his finger – purchased with a shilling which had recently been given to him. Some of the astonished children we regret to chronicle, set up a shout, "Ballington's a backslider!" and for a moment a scene of confusion reigned at the tea table. Then the voice of the General was heard, loud, deadly, and authoritative: "Silence! His mother will deal with him later." The meal proceeded awkwardly, and when it was over Ballington was closeted for some ten minutes with his mother. "He came out from the interview," says Miss Short, "with very red eyes and without the ring."

When the last baby, Lucy, was born in 1867 [actually, April 28, 1868 —ed.], the General informed the other children of this event in the following manner: "Now, listen; I have got a wonderful piece of news for you. God has sent us a most beautiful present."

At once there was a shout, "Is it alive?"

"Yes," said the General, "it's alive."

"Is it a dog?"

"No."

"A donkey?"

"No."

After a few more guesses at livestock, the General said, with great impressiveness, "It's a baby!"

There was a shout for joy, an instant demand to see the newcomer, and then the children crept upstairs after their father, on tiptoe, and were shown the baby. Then Ballington said, "That's what I've been praying for – a baby"; but Miss Short is disposed to think that for some weeks Ballington had been praying industriously for a donkey.

Miss Short cannot remember a single occasion on which theological difficulties, difficulties of faith, were discussed at the Booth table. Although religion entered into every detail of their lives, they never spoke – at any rate before Miss Short – of intellectual problems, all their difficulties lying in the sphere of conduct. To live more perfectly in accord with the Christian spirit, to make other Christians more earnest, to save sinners from temporal wretchedness and everlasting damnation – these were the chief subjects of their table talk. "I think it was the suffering and misery all about them," says Miss Short, "which made the General and his wife stick to the simple elementary truths of religion. I know this, that they had made up their minds to treat the London poor exactly like heathen. It would have been absurd to preach to these poor people about theology; and the General, whose heart was torn by suffering, centered himself on saving their souls. I have heard him preach very beautiful sermons on love, and I remember in particular a sermon on the text, *Acquaint now thyself with Him, and be at peace*, which was as gentle as it was moving; but he used to say, whenever we praised sermons of this kind, 'No; the best preaching is Damnation, with the Cross in the middle of it.' Experience had taught him that. The heathen poor had to be roused to a sense of their danger before they could shake off their spiritual torpor, and even *desire* immortal happiness. I don't think his thoughts ever wandered very far from that center of religion. He believed that the Bible was the inspired Word of God, and in the Bible he found that the injunction to repent preceded the invitation to holiness. No one in his house questioned for a single moment, or in any respect, the truth of the Bible."

As an example of the harrowing effect produced upon William Booth's mind by the destitution and depravity of London, Miss Short relates the story of the first Christmas Day she spent in his home. "The General," she says, "had determined that the children should have a thoroughly happy old-fashioned Christmas, and for a week beforehand every preparation was made for a great family festival. The children were full of excitement, their father entered into the spirit of the thing, and I really thought it would be a day of the purest happiness. But when the General returned from his preaching in Whitechapel on Christmas morning, he was pale, haggard, and morose. He did his best to enter into the children's fun and frolic, but it was no use; he kept relapsing into silence and gloom. He looked dreadfully white and drawn, just as if he were ill or harassed by some grievous worry. And then suddenly he burst out, 'I'll never have a Christmas Day like this again!' and, getting on his feet and walking up and down the room like a caged lion, he told us of the sights he had seen that morning in Whitechapel, indignantly saying, 'The poor have nothing but the public house – nothing but the public house!' I remembered how he had once stopped me at every public house on the Mile End Road, pointing to the young men and women, who crowded the different bars, exclaiming, 'Look at that! – look at it! – enough to make the angels weep!' Sights of this kind, which other people would see and regret, seemed to stab him to the heart; other people only saw the drinking, he saw the poverty, the misery, the disease, and the godlessness behind it; the sins of London didn't shock him, they seemed to tear at his heart with claws that drew blood.

Well, he was true to his word. That Christmas Day was the last Christmas Day the Booth family ever spent together. On the following Christmas Day we were scattered in the slums distributing plum puddings. I remember that we thought the Mission a very great affair because we gave away 150 puddings! How little any of us foresaw the future. Last year the Army distributed 30,000 puddings in London alone! All the same, our little gift of 150, many of them made in the kitchen on Gore Road, was the beginning of the Salvation Army's Christmas Day. The General said to me one day, after a prayer meeting, at which some of the recipients had been blessed, 'Sister Jane, the Lord accepted our puddings.'"

Distressed as he was by the penury and degradation of East London, William Booth was never morose when working to change the souls of men. Miss Short says he would carry a meeting before him by his humor and his hopefulness; and the more miserable and broken-hearted his audience, the more cheerfulness he put into his methods. She remembers that he was preaching once in a hall for the first time under a sounding board – a very heavy and clumsy contrivance which hung just over his head. At the end of his address he invited men to come and testify on the platform, adding, "But only those who are really saved had better come, for"– pointing to the sounding board, "it may mean death." It was such remarks as this, startling in those days, which endeared him to his rough audiences, who were sharply conscious of sanctimoniousness.

He was, nevertheless, still a trifle clerical, for on one occasion when a converted laborer desired to preach, he insisted that the man should wear a black suit of clothes, and actually gave the convert his only other suit, frock coat and all, in which the new preacher cut a sufficiently comical figure. It would be explained later on that only after many rebuffs from the churches did he strike out on those original lines which culminated in the Salvation Army.

His great secret of success, Miss Short is quite certain, was the discovery of the enormous influence of love and kindness in dealing with fallen humanity. Very early in those first years in London, he showed boundless compassion to a man sunk in misery and sin, hunting his soul with the "deliberate speed, majestic instancy" of the Hound of Heaven. And when the man yielded at last, it was the astonished exclamation, "Love and kindness! Then there really is a God."

"There were many disappointments," says Miss Short, "some of them enough to embitter any man; but he never lost heart, although these disappointments caused him dreadful pain at the time. One of his evangelists went wrong, and for days he found it impossible to shake off the sorrow caused by this fall. Then there was a young man who worked for him, and whom he loved, a young man with what you might call a storybook face – so handsome, heroic, and pure. One day they came and told the General that this young man was in the London Hospital with a serious injury to his spine; although he shrank from seeing this friend in pain, he posted off at once, and when he arrived it was to hear a confession of embezzlement. He knelt down at the bedside, before the whole ward, and prayed for the soul of that young man, his own heart utterly miserable. But in this case he was made happy by the restoration of the injured youth, who took his advice, made a full confession of his crime, and repaid every penny of the money. That, as you probably know, was one of General Booth's strictest rules. Repentance meant confession and restoration. This teaching sent many a man to prison whose crime would never have been discovered, and many more he sent to their employers, often going with them, to confess the sins of which they had been guilty."

Of his stern honesty with himself Miss Short does not entertain the shadow of a doubt. "You can see how honest he was by his relations with Mr. Henry Reed, the very rich Australian living in Tunbridge Wells who came under the spell of Mr. Booth's preaching. I can distinctly remember the joy and the hope with which the General set out on one of his journeys to Dunorlan, Mr. Reed's beautiful place in Tunbridge Wells, believing that he would come back with hundreds of pounds towards the three thousand he was striving to raise for a Mission Hall. But he came back, instead, utterly depressed; indeed, I think that was the only occasion on which I ever saw him really dejected. And why was this? It was just because the religious people surrounding Mr. Reed, and who crowded the park to hear the Whitechapel missionary preach, were such 'poor stuff.' I remember how the General walked up and down the room muttering, 'I want men! I want men!'

He doubted all religion that made people soft and selfish. He was very suspicious of any religion which did not develop into work for others. The people he met that day thought too much of dogma and too little of Christian service – they didn't hunger and thirst after the saving of lost souls. Mr. Reed offered the General a lot of money, and if I remember rightly a suitable site in East London, and a fine hall that was to cost something like seven thousand pounds. But after making this splendid offer, which took the General's breath away, Mr. Reed explained that the Mission in the future must be conducted in a manner of which he approved, making it quite clear that he expected to exercise authority over the General. A weaker man than the General might have been tempted to accept this splendid gift on any terms, but the General was far too honest a man to prevaricate for a moment. He rejected the offer. He refused to put himself under the dominion of a sect. But I really think he was more dejected by the spirit of the Christianity he encountered in Tunbridge Wells than by the loss of this tremendously large sum of money. He kept on saying, 'I want men! I want men!'. . . "

It would be possible, perhaps, for an unscrupulous writer in years to come, when witnesses for the defense are dead, to accuse William Booth of something like harshness towards his children; to suggest, at any rate, that he was a man who preached one life in the pulpit and did not quite practice it in his home. We do not pretend for a moment that he was faultless; we readily deplore in him the absence of some of those refinements of nature which are the marks of genuine sainthood; he was not perhaps as gentle as we would wish a hero of religion to be; he lacked something of that fathomless humility, that unbounded reverence for childhood, and that inexhaustible tolerance for the weaknesses of human nature which endear the holiest of men to the affections of mortality.

But enough has been said in this place to prevent his exhibition, even with these faults, as anything but a true and affectionate father. He was not one thing in the pulpit and another in his home; he was never in such a relation to his children as made them distrust or fear him. Those occasional explosions which characterized him all his life, and which malignity might exaggerate, were never taken very seriously either by his children or his followers. They sprang from physical disabilities, from dyspepsia, and from the attacks of neuralgia which repeatedly racked his nerves; and they were short-lived. He was a man who never sulked. Suddenly he would blaze into anger, with all the appearance of fiery indignation, and at the next moment he would be laughing at himself, or rallying with generous humor the victim of his reproof.

Bramwell Booth, whose reverence for his father is well known, and on whom that father leaned almost alone in the years of widowerhood, is honest and fearless enough to say that he considers his father did thrash him on several occasions without justice. At the same time he scoffs out of hearing the least suggestion that his father was despotic or unkind. "We adored him!" he exclaims; "every one of us; and, even when we sulked, we were always longing for his forgiveness."

Miss Short's testimony is to the like effect. "When elder children were in trouble it was usually to their father, not to their mother, that they would go. I remember one day that Emma had a bad fit, after squashing her finger very badly in one of the doors; she lay sobbing on the floor, refusing to be comforted, till her father rushed upstairs, threw himself on the floor beside her, gathered her into his arms, and mothered her with all the tenderness of a woman. He was impatient with them at times, particularly when he was bowed down by worries, but he loved them most dearly. One day he was dictating a number of letters to me in his room, when one of the girls entered, went to the piano, and sat down to practice her scales. Mrs. Booth was lying down in the next room, ill and nervous. He jumped up, seized the child in his hands, rated her soundly for not thinking of her mother, and then pushed her sharply out of the room. On that occasion he was distinctly angry, and it pained me to see the child treated so roughly. But a minute or two afterwards Mrs. Booth entered the room. 'William,' she said reproachfully, 'it was kind of you to think of me, but I am sorry you should ———' In an instant he was on his feet, with his arms round her, and I slipped from the room. He could repent with all the abandonment of a child."

No one, says Miss Short, can possibly understand William Booth who does not realize that he was of a most energetic and enthusiastic nature. "I have never met any one," she declares, "who could compare with him in any way in this respect. And as he was an extraordinarily pure man, loathing and abominating anything that was the least coarse – his purity of mind, heart, and soul struck me greatly – you can see that the force of his nature would drive him furiously through the day's work. He was always facing in the one direction. The day could never be too long for what he had to do. And nobody, I'm afraid, could ever be quick enough and intelligent enough to keep up with him. I know that he broke me down! Mrs. Booth herself warned me on several occasions that if I let him he would kill me; and indeed I had to go away at last, and take a long sea voyage, to recover even a fraction of my former health."

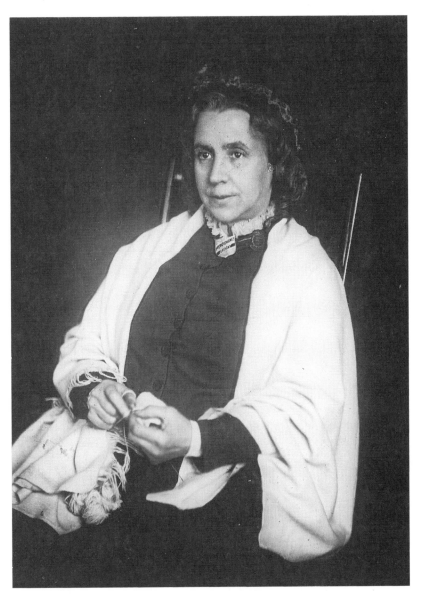

I shall never forget the General's love for his wife.

FATHER AND SON

Bramwell Booth

Echoes and Memories (London: Hodder & Stoughton, 1925)

William Bramwell Booth (1856-1929) was the eldest son of William and Catherine Booth. He was nine years old when his parents started The Christian Mission and twenty-two when it became The Salvation Army. He was, therefore, old enough to experience the beginnings and mature enough to become his father's chief assistant when the transition to a military organization was made in 1878. He remained the Chief of Staff until he became General when his father died in 1912. He therefore knew his father better than anyone else, except his mother. His recollection contained in his memoirs is tender but not eulogistic;Bramwell recognized that his father had some human frailties and, though a great man, was, happily, not perfect.

One picture among the many that I cherish of my father I should like to place at the very beginning of what I have to say of him here. It explains a certain new development in the history of the Army, but it also gives a glimpse of the deep fires that burned in the personality of William Booth. One morning, away back in the eighties, I was an early caller at his house in Clapton. Here I found him in his dressing room, preparing for the day with ferocious energy. The hairbrushes which he held in either hand were being wielded with quite eloquent vigor upon a mane that was more refractory than usual, and his braces were flying like the wings of Pegasus. No good-morning-how-do-you-do here!

"Bramwell," he cried, when he caught sight of me, "did you know that men slept out all night on the bridges?"

He had arrived in London very late the night before from some town in the south of England, and had to cross the city to reach his home.

What he had seen on that midnight return accounted for this morning tornado. Did I know that men slept out all night on the bridges?

"Well, yes," I replied, "a lot of poor fellows, I suppose, do that."

"Then you ought to be ashamed of yourself to have known it and done nothing for them," he went on vehemently.

I began to speak of the difficulties, burdened as we were already, of taking up all sorts of Poor Law work, and so forth. My father stopped me with a peremptory wave of the brushes.

"Go and do something!" he said. "We *must* do something."

"What can we do?"

"Get them a shelter!"

"That will cost money."

"Well, that is your affair! Something must be done. Get hold of a warehouse and warm it, and find something to cover them. But mind, Bramwell, no coddling!"

That was the beginning of The Salvation Army shelters, the earliest and most typical institutions connected with our now worldwide social work. But it also throws a ray of light on the characteristic benevolence of the Army's founder. Benevolence, which is a languid quality in many men, with him was passionate. I should be disposed to place his benevolence first among his characteristics. I write of him here, as far as it is possible to do so, aside from what I humbly acknowledge to have been the great determining force of his life – namely the uplifting and guiding influence of the Spirit of God. This apart, his benevolence was the first quality to light up. The governing influence of his life was goodwill to his fellows. I am not saying that he never thought of himself. His saintship was not after the pattern of Francis d'Assisi, at least as described by Paul Sabatier. Nor can I say that he was always at the same level of self-denial and self-effacement in order to give practical expression to his benevolent impulse. But I do say, looking at his life as I saw it over a great span of years, not only in workday association as his comrade and principal helper, but in the still closer intimacy of a son, that his benevolence was the leading feature of his character. He really set out to do good to all men – an object which, no doubt, often seemed hopeless, but not on that account to be less sought after. The horizon of his soul was not limited by human hope – it reached out to divine power and love. His heart was a bottomless well of compassion, and it was for this reason principally that, although perhaps more widely and persistently abused than any other figure of his time, he was even more widely and tenaciously loved.

It would be easy to multiply evidences of his own unselfishness. The slander that he enriched himself was not merely untrue, it was ridiculously untrue. It was not merely a distortion of the facts, it was an inversion of them. Again and again he had legitimate opportunities to enrich himself, and no one would have flung a stone at him had he accepted them, but he turned them down without hesitating a moment. Rich men even sent him blank checks on condition that the amount which he filled in should apply to his own personal use. The checks were returned. For the Army he was ready to accept such gifts with both hands, for himself, not at all.

Next to this, his outstanding qualities – and, indeed, I am always in doubt whether it should not be placed first – was his temperamental simplicity. If his appearance, with his smooth and open forehead, his kindling and flashing eyes, his "eminent" nose, his shaggy visage, his general expression of keenness and vivacity, suggested some ancient prophet, his heart was the heart of a little child. His guilelessness was one great secret of his strength. Many who came into his presence were so impressed by his openness and candor, the absence of all pretense and casuistry, that they went away feeling that if they had a thousand lives they could trust them into his hands.

This simplicity of character, of course, had its apparent disadvantages. He would often say what everyone thought to be impolitic. The fear of his occasional imprudence gave me bad half hours! There were interviews of great importance, for example, when it was certainly the part of worldly, if not of spiritual wisdom to refrain from entering upon certain subjects so long as silence could be maintained with honor. In such circumstances he was never to be trusted, however much he might have been entreated beforehand! The interview would be half through, when out would come the cat from the bag. It was delightful, and I am bound to say that I never – or very rarely – found anything but good come of his "indiscretions," however much they might give me and others "pins and needles" at the time.

In the same way, if, in urging any particular course upon others, he had any second intention, something at the back of his mind – any *arrière-pensée*, as the saying is – it was sure to make its appearance before the parley ended. He could not have kept it back.

Anything "put on" or "made-up" was anathema. His honesty was not on the infamous copy-book maxim. Had he been a thief – and he was in the habit of saying that by nature he was a grabber! – he would have been a shining example of the honor which is supposed to exist among the fraternity! Nor was he honest only because his religion made him so, although, of course, his religion fortified him in his honesty. But sincerity was a native quality with him. It was in the mold from which he was taken. If it were possible to think of William Booth without his religion, such a William Booth would certainly have been a sincere and honest man.

The third outstanding characteristic in him was his granite and superlative will. He was immovable, and therefore, in the passive sense, invincible. Anything like slackness or wobbling or unsteadiness in purpose was abhorred. When he had considered a matter, and made up his mind about it, not all the angels of heaven could have shaken his determination. This led him at times upon a line of conduct which may have appeared pedantic to those who did not understand; yet one could never forget that it was this strength in him which enabled him to achieve so much. His determined and steadfast will was really the driving force of his other qualities.

It was these three characteristics in combination which distinguished his personality and set him apart in his generation. Other men, no doubt, have had equal power of will, but without his genius for compassion; others, again, may have a like simplicity, but without the indomitable will. It was his will power which directed his other qualities to practical ends. Without it he would still have been splendid and most lovable, but he would not have been the founder of The Salvation Army.

He had, I dare say, the faults of these qualities. His own benevolence made him impatient of the selfish and, perhaps, too swift in his judgment of those who only cared to gratify themselves. He was at times a hasty executioner, deaf to excuses until after the culprit's head was off!

His sincerity, too, as I have already hinted, had its embarrassing side. In writing of W.E. Gladstone, Lord Morley said that "He had a marked habit of believing people; it was part of his simplicity." Well, so with my father. He believed people. He was so utterly sincere himself that he could not credit that others could practice any deception. It was only with the greatest difficulty, and in face of the most unquestionable evidence, that he would accept the fact that he had been intentionally misled or treated unfairly. In the official life of the Army, long after he should have let people go, in the interests of the Army itself, he persisted in holding on to them. It was not a mere polite reluctance to believe that men were not honorable and straightforward; it was almost a constitutional inability.

His great will power, again, at times made him difficult to deal with. His own determination clashed with the determination of others, and the sudden friction produced sparks; not often, fortunately, leading to conflagration, though sometimes these did happen. No doubt, there was a vein of hardness in him. It ran side by side with a vein of exquisite tenderness. But the hardness was there. Had it not been there he could not have accomplished what he did. Weakness always fails.

It is impossible to speak of my father in this intimate way without some estimate of the influence of my mother upon him. That influence was extraordinarily uplifting and encouraging, especially during the early years of the movement, when he was liable to depression and to a sense of loneliness, both of which wore off, in some measure, as the success of the work became assured. Catherine Booth continually fed his enthusiasm with fresh fuel, strengthened his faith in God, and pointed him to the gleaming distance. She was the complement of him as he was of her. Marvelously did they fit into one another. Where his temperament was unsure, she was buoyant; where she would waver, he was a rock. Both of them, I dare say, had faults, his a certain superficial irritability, especially when worn and tried; hers the inclination to take the less hopeful view on certain matters. But the faults of each other were wonderfully neutralized in the personality of the other.

In some ways she was more combative than he. She was, for example, more inclined to resent the injustices to which, especially, again in the early days, the Army was continually subject. He was rather content to let such opposition tire itself out, and to answer misrepresentation with silence, because he feared that to turn aside upon these guerilla engagements would be to weaken the Army for the real fight against the hosts of the devil, who held captive the souls of men. He used to say, "Better to suffer than contend." But her counsel was ever, "Up and at them, William!" She was a warrior; of compromise she would have none.

Their relationship during all the thirty years that I had them together was ideal. His love for her was entirely beautiful – something quite out of the ordinary, even in the happiest unions. Mingled with his love was an element of deep admiration for her uncommon ability. She was far more widely read than he. Certain circumstances of her youth had favored what was a naturally studious temperament, and her spiritual influence, her devotion to Jesus Christ, her intense longings for the advance of His Kingdom on earth, her intellectual skill, her command of widely gathered information helped him in his hurried and stormy life to look beyond his own immediate interests and ideas, and to look on to that City which hath foundations. Speaking beside her open grave, he said:

I have never turned from her these forty years for any journeying on my mission of mercy, but I longed to get back, and have counted the weeks, days, and hours which should take me again to her side. When she has gone away from me it has been just the same. And now she has gone away for the last time. What then is there left for me to do? Not to count the weeks, the days, and the hours which shall bring me again into her sweet company, seeing that I know not what will be on the morrow, nor what an hour may bring forth. My work plainly is to fill up the weeks, the days, the hours, and cheer my poor heart as I go along with the thought that when I have served my Christ and my generation according to the will of God, which I vow this afternoon I will to the last drop of my blood – then I trust that she will bid me welcome to the Skies as he bade her.

Her delicacy of health, which was the heritage of spinal trouble in her girlhood, unfitted her in some respects to be the wife of a poor minister, whose income was scarcely sufficient to cover the domestic needs. There is an undertone in some of her letters to him before their marriage which suggests that she could see him occupying a very different station, and one worthier of the powers she already knew him to possess. In my boyhood I have sometimes known her exceedingly harassed by the cares of a house full of children, and tried, no doubt, by difficult circumstances, and by her own bodily weakness. I have seen him come into the house, put his hat down in the hall, and, entering the room, find it all out in a moment. Taking her hand, he would say, "Kate, let me pray with you," and he would turn us out while they knelt together. Then a little while later it was evident that the skies were blue again.

Although he was at times irascible, and, when displeased, had great liberty of speech, I never heard him in all those long years – many of them years of intense strain upon them both, with all the demands which poverty and sickness made upon patience and kindness in the home – say one harsh word to her. There were times when he would arrive at the house like a hurricane, blowing, as it were, the children right and left – we used to call him the "Bishop" in those early days, and sometimes, although we loved the very ground he trod upon, we were unanimously agreed on the advisability of keeping out of the way of his "visitations" – but to her he would be like a lover of twenty come to visit his girl!

I touch with hesitation the subject of my father's religion. How, indeed, can it be dealt with in a page of reminiscence! But, at least, this may be said: that it was never a platform pose. The religion he commended to his fellows with such directness and sincerity was the religion which he himself accepted with all his heart and lived with all his might. And it was a success. It sustained especially in those later years when he was sorrow-stricken and really heartbroken by the loss of those he loved. I do not suggest that he was always shouting the praises of God at the top of his voice to his housekeeper, but I do say that amid all the innumerable affairs of his crowded life the vision of a mighty

God, and of a present Savior, was ever before him – was ever the great possession of his soul – that he had a fine consciousness of the responsibility to God for every gift he possessed and a profound sense of eternal things.

Despite his wonderful capacity of eliciting the emotions of others, often playing upon them as a harper upon the strings, he was singularly reticent about his own inner life. He was totally innocent of "gush." Yet who knew him that could doubt the reality of his spiritual experience? It sustained him amid persecutions, slanders, and conflicts, and under the burden of a world of cares such as few men have been called to endure. It did more than sustain him in the stoic sense; it kept his spirit sweet. When I have gone to him, perhaps with some infamous newspaper attack, and in my indignation have said, "This is really more than we can stand," he has replied, "Bramwell, fifty years hence it will matter very little indeed how these people treated us; it will matter a great deal how we dealt with the work of God." He would not accuse those who accused him. He would not impugn the motives or imply evil. He could speak out when duty demanded. But he did not wish to speak. He would never take unfair advantage in argument or treat personalities as reasons. He rather strove to account for the mistakes of his opponents, and to hope all things. It was his rule not to retaliate, scarcely to explain, and it was perfectly delightful to see how many cursings and railings turned out in the end to be blessings. There is a story of one of our Canadian officers who, on being pelted with eggs, found that by some mistake of the mob the eggs were quite good, and, deftly catching them, she presently turned them into omelettes!

That was William Booth all over!

William Booth at work with his son Bramwell

THE SIMPLE LIFE

J. Evan Smith
in *Booth the Beloved* (London: OUP, 1949): 10-19.

William Booth was fortunate throughout his career to have had intelligent and capable confidantes, some of whose contributions to the Army's success have not been fully acknowledged. Among the most trusted, though without much power, were his private secretaries, men like Fred Cox and J. Evan Smith. These were the men who, in his later years, not only wrote his letters but took care of his personal needs and were ever at hand to answer his beck and call. J. Evan Smith, as a young Lieutenant, became William Booth's "confidential stenographer" or private secretary in 1907 and retained that position until William Booth died in August 1912. He, therefore, had the opportunity to become well acquainted with the personal habits and tastes of the General. These he describes vividly and with good humor in his autobiography published in 1949.

Intimate association with William Booth – bound up as I was with his private life – enabled me to study him closely, and it is worthy of note that the characteristics for which this one-time pawnbroker's assistant ultimately became world renowned in his public service were equally in evidence in his life behind the scenes.

William Booth's habits were plain and simple in the extreme. Although by this time he could have commanded the best of everything, and could have personally benefited by the numerous gifts, both in money and kind, that wealthy people were ready to shower upon him, he steadfastly refused to accept anything in the nature of presents for himself. All had to go into the Army pool.

A friend once laughingly suggested to the General that his success, and the universal respect in which he was held would turn his head.

"You will be getting a swelled head in your old age," he said. The old man answered quite simply – his birthday had just passed: "All yesterday I was overwhelmed with telegrams and letters of congratulations from all quarters of the world. My only feeling was one of intense humility, which could find no more adequate expression than in the old phrase, 'Oh, Lord, thou knowest I am the least of all Thy saints.'"

That, indeed, was his attitude to the end. He viewed himself but as an instrument in the hands of a greater force than he.

As one remembers this conception of his work, one understands a little better the great simplicity and singleness of purpose of his life. He was encumbered very little with possessions.

His residence at Hadley Wood, rented to him by the Army, was a very modest home; the General's study and bedroom being the best of the half dozen main rooms, which also included the secretary's office and bedroom, a small dining room, and sleeping accommodations for the housekeeper and her assistant.

He had no hobbies or recreations. His physical exercise was obtained by a brief walk around the garden or along the country lanes surrounding the house.

Had there been a conveyance to take him to the railway station when going on a journey, this patriarch of eighty years would have considered it extravagant to have indulged for that relatively short distance. Hurrying down the avenue to catch the train, nipped sometimes by the biting wind, he would stop at distances of between fifty and sixty yards in order to regain his breath, leaning heavily upon my shoulder in the meantime.

His antipathy to unnecessary expenditure sometimes caused his personal staff considerable concern. They felt that at his age and with the great burdens resting upon him, nothing that would contribute to his personal comfort should be withheld. But he was not to be moved. The call to service was always more important to him than consideration of physical infirmity, and the needs of the poor and outcast had constant priority in his thoughts.

When he was in England on Christmas Day he delighted to visit the various social institutions. There was obvious joy and satisfaction in his heart as he went from place to place, seeing the careworn and poverty stricken partaking of a hot Christmas dinner. This, he felt, was the best way for money to be spent; not on him – never on him!

His frugal habits were perhaps most noticeable in the simplicity of his diet. He often said that many people ate themselves to death, and considered that a well-chosen diet contributed to longevity.

When accepting hospitality it was customary, to prevent the hostess going to unnecessary trouble, to forward as a guideline a suggested menu, which indicated that the General did not take fish, flesh or fowl in any shape or form. Here is the first part of one such letter:

Dear Friend,

I am informed that you have very kindly undertaken to entertain General Booth during his visit to your town, and, as his requirements are somewhat unusual – though very simple – we feel sure you will welcome the information as to his needs which we have the pleasure to give below.

The General does not take fish, flesh or fowl in any shape or form.

Tea, about 4:30: Strong Ceylon tea, boiling hot milk, white bread, dry toast and butter, with the addition of a few fried potatoes (or mushrooms, if convenient).

In making the toast, the bread should be cut tolerably thin, and gradually toasted until it is both dry and crisp, and yet not too hard, and should be then immediately placed in the rack.

If, however, for some reason or other the letter was not dispatched, the General made no change in his habits.

When entertained by a doctor the General liked to chaff his host on the subject of dieting. While others of us were enjoying a good square meal and he was having toast and tea, he would suddenly turn upon his host and ask peremptorily, "Doctor, why don't you diet your patients?" If the doctor looked embarrassed and lost for a reply, the General would say, whimsically, "Shall I tell you why? If you did you would lose your practice altogether!"

When visiting the city of Paisley for a special meeting he was entertained by Sir James Coats, of the noted cotton manufacturing firm, and

Lady Coats, at their beautiful home. A sumptuous repast had been prepared for the distinguished guest, and as we sat down at the table the hostess quoted from the menu – soup, fish, pheasant, vegetables, sweets, etc. – but when she asked the General what he would take he astonished her by replying, "Not of that for me, thank you, Lady Coats. Will you please ask the maid to bring me a bowl of bread and milk?" I may say that I made up for him.

His favorite drink was strong tea, diluted with plenty of boiled milk, and this he insisted should be served really hot. If lukewarm he would not complain to the hostess, but turn to the maid, standing by, and, with his hand encircling the cup, call out in his deepest tones, "Mary" (he called all the maids, "Mary"), "Mary, I like my tea as I like my religion – *hot, very hot.*"

The General's good health and longevity were a testimony to the wisdom of dieting. When he dilated upon the subject no one could oppose him for long, because his extraordinary energy and alertness of mind and body were indisputable proofs that his abstemiousness did not militate against his vigor. Nevertheless, he was constantly having advice tendered him, especially by his hosts.

When detained by very late meetings in the west of London the General would sometimes accept the hospitality of the Hon. Mrs. O'Grady, sister of Admiral of the Fleet Lord Charles Beresford. There was still considerable controversy about the justification of the Boer War, and on this subject her ladyship and the General had warm discussions. Mrs. O'Grady, however, was greatly concerned about the General's health, and once, when saying good-bye to him in the vestibule of her home, she turned to me and said, "Now look after the General, and (confidentially) try to persuade him at lunchtime each day to take a *glass of port*," adding with emphasis, *"you see, it makes blood!"*

The idea of suggesting such a course to the Founder of the greatest temperance organization in the world was very amusing. I never attempted it.

The General's attitude toward his wearing apparel sometimes afforded us not a little amusement. Occasionally he would complain that his underwear, which in variable seasons had to be frequently changed, was being worn threadbare by its rough treatment at the laundry.

Though in the matter of personal cleanliness he was most fastidious, when this had been in use for only a day or two, an airing by the window, he jokingly suggested, should suffice!

He was, too, very reluctant to part with his old clothes. Of some he was particularly fond, especially so of a wellworn dressing gown. But once, when were absent on a tour, his son, Bramwell, went to his room and removed a number of his shabby garments – the dressing gown among them. When the General returned it could not, of course, be found, and on inquiring from the housekeeper, she had to confess what had happened.

When next the Chief called upon his father he was challenged with some warmth: "Bramwell," he said, "what have you been doing with my old clothes?"

"Oh," replied the Chief, knowing his father's compassion for the poor, and thinking he had an excellent excuse, "I thought they were really getting too bad for you to wear, and that some of the poor fellows down at the shelter would be glad to have them." Whereupon the old gentleman, seeing through this little stratagem, immediately and vigorously responded, "Look here, Bramwell, you leave my things alone and do your charities at your own expense!"

The General had no appointed hairdresser, averring that my clip was quite satisfactory. Sitting on a chair in the middle of his study, over the carpet of which I had first spread a large white sheet, and with another such around his shoulders and tucked into his neck, I would amateurishly perform my allotted task, interrupted only by occasional directions from my esteemed "customer," or shall I say "sufferer"?

Half an hour's sleep following his midday meal was an unfailing necessity if the General were to be kept on his feet, and the absolute quietude required for this was not always easy to obtain, especially in certain places where we were accomodated.

Lady Inskip has reminded me that when she was very small they had a nursery right at the top of their house. General Booth and his secretary came to stay with them for a while, and occupied the floor midway between the bottom and top of the house. Her ladyship said that she very vividly remembered being confronted with a huge notice, "Hush! The General sleeps," which was pinned upon the door.

"Needless to say, we were all very quiet," she added.

One of my most difficult tasks was to copy out the notes which the General himself could not be bothered to decipher. Commissioner Scott Railton had a good facility for writing and had an easy style. His handwriting, however, was atrocious and the General could make neither heads nor tails of it, so I had to work at it and type copies, so that the General could read it easily. The Commissioner's writing was like that of many doctors, who seem to make their writing nearly indecipherable by intent.

William Booth was an indefatigable worker. It would be difficult to discover in the long catalogue of historic personalities one who wasted less time. His passion to put every moment to use seemed to increase rather than to decrease with the passing of the years.

Never was he idle, nor could he tolerate seeing anyone else idle, as those of his personal staff well knew. He had no room for slackers. He coined a phrase, *"Every hour and every power for Christ and duty,"* and that was never more true of anyone than of the man himself. He toiled night and day, dictated letters and messages, gave important decisions, interviewed prominent people, prepared sermons and articles for the press, at home, in the office, on board ship and in cab or car, messages which I was expected to type under the strangest circumstances. Business was transacted during our travels in respect to prominent Army leaders and the activities of the organization in all parts of the world. Often I have typed letters with the machine on the seat of a railway compartment, while I knelt on the floor, tapping out the words with considerable difficulty.

He felt irritated if he had to spend time changing trains and waiting about for an hour or two before he could continue his journey. "Why," he would ask, "could they not have arranged a meeting for me?"

To get the Founder to the railway station more than five minutes before the train was due to leave was a sad error, for this would necessitate his pacing up and down the platform or sitting more or less idly in the compartment waiting for the train to start. In such an unfortunate circumstance the General would express himself freely, something along these lines: "Now you're happy – having got me here too soon.

What will these people think of me wasting my time like this? They'll think I've nothing else to do."

On these travels I carried a portable electric bell. Upon arrival at our guest house this was placed in my bedroom and the lengthy piece of flex was extended to the General's room, the bell push being fixed at the head of the bed near at hand, so that he could ring should he require me during the night.

Sometimes, when in a highly nervous state, the General would have long periods of wakefulness, and many, in consequence, would be the calls made upon me. When the bell rang I would jump out of bed, don a dressing gown, fumble around for my shorthand book and pencil, and stumble into his room half asleep, to take down some of the profound thoughts that had come to him during the wakeful hours of the night. I often wished he would have fewer thoughts at night and thus permit me to have more unbroken sleep. But on occasion that bell would ring two, three, four and even five and six times a night – such was the restlessness of the old warhorse.

When there was no electric light to switch on and off the General found his repeater watch useful in the darkness of the night. When he awoke he would move a lever with his thumb and the watch would chime while he listened intently – one note for every hour and another for each five minutes.

At this time the Founder rarely went to his office at international headquarters, and when not campaigning did most of his work at home.

When, however, there was something of particular importance requiring his attention we would go together by train from Hadley Wood Station to King's Cross, and then take a hansom cab, or a "growler," as the four-wheeled horse-drawn cab was called, to the office on Queen Victoria Street.

There the General would be fully and closely occupied with important matters of business, including lengthy interviews with the chief of the staff and his leading commissioners, with Sir Washington Ranger and Mr. W. Frost, the Army's lawyers, or perhaps with some well-known personality, having no respite, except for a meager lunch and his accustomed half-hour rest. For this I would lead him to the room below his office, which was equipped with a comfortable bed and closed off, so as to make possible the essential "forty winks."

One essential of our traveling equipment was folds of black cloth and drawing pins. The General was a very light sleeper, and upon arriving at our destination it was necessary to adjust things in the bedroom in such a way as would be conducive to his comfort and rest. The slightest chink of light streaming through the window at dawn would be sufficient to wake him, so it was necessary to cover the windows with this black material and effectively darken the room. Sometimes this presented a real difficulty. I did not want to make any more fuss than was necessary by disturbing the host or hostess, and so would get a chair, or, if in a large mansion where windows were high and wide, I would have to clamber up on a table or dresser, stretching up to fix the drawing pins, seeing to it that every likely glimmer of light was eliminated. Unpleasant accidents and bad bruises were not a few!

The bed then would be made up and the pillows suitably fixed, placed back to the window, or the bed itself turned around, and other preparations made for the night, including the fixing of the portable electric bell push.

To persuade him to take a holiday was nearly impossible, though someone was always trying. In the city of Liverpool lived a wealthy maiden lady who was keenly interested in the work of The Salvation Army and who became one of its most generous supporters. The General visited her delightful home whenever possible to talk with her about his pet schemes, as a result of which he anticipated receiving substantial donations to give effect to them. In this he was not disappointed. But, concerned because she felt the General was working far too hard, this lady said to him on one occasion, "General, if only you will take a holiday" – he had said he had not taken a holiday for more than twenty years – "I'll place at your disposal my house" – a beautiful mansion – "and my horses and carriages, and, in addition, I'll give you five thousand pounds for that new scheme of yours."

Well do I recollect the General repeating to me what she had said, and how whimsically he observed, "Smith, I'm not taking a holiday, but I'm after that five thousand pounds all the same." He got it, too, and more besides!

Indeed, he begrudged even an hour away from his work. Once he was persuaded to have a party for the benefit of his grandchildren, for whom he reluctantly spared an hour or two of his precious time.

Commissioner and Mrs. Booth-Tucker, I remember, and the Chief, as he was known, and Mrs. Bramwell Booth, with several of their children, gathered in the Founder's study. What a party it was! There were no games, Christmas packets or bumper packages, but the singing of well-known Army choruses and testimonies from the grandchildren.

There was, too, some free and happy conversation between the items, but all the while the old gentleman was itching to get back to work. While one of the grandchildren was singing, this inveterate toiler suddenly emerged from the study and came to my office, saying, "Smith, I wish we could get on with our work!"

That work was for him an obsession, and it is perfectly true that he did not lift his finger from the pulse of the worldwide affairs of the Army until he passed to his heavenly reward.

William Booth with his daughter Evangeline

CREST BOOKS
The Salvation Army National Publications

Shaw Clifton, *Never the Same Again: Encouragement for new and not–so–new Christians*, 1997

Compilation, *Christmas Through the Years: A War Cry Treasury*, 1997

William Francis, *Celebrate the Feasts of the Lord: The Christian Heritage of the Sacred Jewish Festivals*, 1998

Marlene Chase, *Pictures from the Word*, 1998

Joe Noland, *A Little Greatness*, 1998

Lyell M. Rader, *Romance & Dynamite: Essays on Science & the Nature of Faith*, 1998

Shaw Clifton, *Who Are These Salvationists? An Analysis for the 21st Century*, 1999

Compilation, *Easter Through the Years: A War Cry Treasury*, 1999

Terry Camsey, *Slightly Off Center! Growth Principles to Thaw Frozen Paradigms*, 2000

Philip Needham, *He Who Laughed First: Delighting in a Holy God*, (in collaboration with Beacon Hill Press, Kansas City), 2000

Henry Gariepy, ed., *A Salvationist Treasury: 365 Devotional Meditations from the Classics to the Contemporary*, 2000

Marlene Chase, *Our God Comes: And Will Not Be Silent*, 2001

A. Kenneth Wilson, *Fractured Parables: And Other Tales to Lighten the Heart and Quicken the Spirit*, 2001

Carroll Ferguson Hunt, *If Two Shall Agree*, (in collaboration with Beacon Hill Press, Kansas City), 2001

John C. Izzard, *Pen of Flame: The Life and Poetry of Catherine Baird*, 2002

Henry Gariepy, *Andy Miller: A Legend and a Legacy*, 2002

Compilation, *A Word in Season: A Collection of Short Stories*, 2002

R. David Rightmire, *Sanctified Sanity: The Life and Teaching of Samuel Logan Brengle*, 2003

Chick Yuill, *Leadership on the Axis of Change*, 2003

Compilation, *Living Portraits Speaking Still: A Collection of Bible Studies*, 2004

A. Kenneth Wilson, *The First Dysfunctional Family: A Modern Guide to the Book of Genesis*, 2004

Allen Satterlee, *Turning Points: How The Salvation Army Found a Different Path*, 2004

David Laeger, *Shadow and Substance: The Tabernacle of the Human Heart*, 2005

Check Yee, *Good Morning China*, 2005

Marlene Chase, *Beside Still Waters: Great Prayers of the Bible for Today*, 2005

Roger J. Green, *The Life & Ministry of William Booth*, (in collaboration with Abingdon Press, Nashville), 2006

Norman H. Murdoch, *Soldiers of the Cross: Pioneers of Social Change*, 2006

Henry Gariepy, *Israel L. Gaither: Man With a Mission*, 2006

R.G. Moyles, *I Knew William Booth: An Album of Remembrances, 2007*